WAR MAKES MEN OF BOYS

NUMBER 140

Williams-Ford Texas A&M University Military History Series

War Makes Men of Boys

A Soldier's World War II

KATHERINE I. MILLER

TEXAS A&M UNIVERSITY PRESS
College Station

First edition

This paper meets the requirements of ANSI / NISO Z39.48-1992.
(Permanence of Paper)
Binding materials have been chosen for durability.

LIBRARY OF CONGRESS CATALOGING-IN-PUBLICATION DATA

Miller, Katherine, 1959–
War makes men of boys : a soldier's World War II / Katherine I. Miller.—1st ed.
p. cm.—(Williams-Ford Texas A&M University military history series ; no. 140)
Includes bibliographical references and index.
ISBN 978-1-60344-770-6 (book/cloth : alk. paper)—ISBN 1-60344-770-9 (book/cloth : alk. paper)—ISBN 978-1-60344-774-4 (ebook)—ISBN 1-60344-774-1 (ebook)—ISBN 978-1-60344-815-4 (book/pbk. : alk. paper)—ISBN 1-60344-815-2 (book/pbk. : alk. paper) 1. Miller, Joe T. (Joe Ted), 1925–2006. 2. Miller, Joe T. (Joe Ted), 1925–2006—Correspondence. 3. Soldiers—United States—Biography. 4. United States. Army. Infantry—Biography. 5. World War, 1939–1945—Veterans—Illinois—Biography. 6. World War, 1939–1945—Personal narratives, American. I. Title. II. Series: Williams-Ford Texas A&M University military history series ; no. 140.
U53.M558M55 2012
940.54'1273092—dc23
[B]

2012016467

To Oscar, Irene, Dorothy, and Judy
his first family

To Margaret
his wife of fifty-three years

To Mary, Barbara, and Ann,
—who, with me, are the family they created—

To Mike, Stosh, Jim, and Gary
the men his daughters married

To Katie, Dan, Samantha, Monika, and Kalena
grandchildren for the future

And most of all
To Bud, and the man he became

CONTENTS

WAR MAKES MEN OF BOYS

PROLOGUE

A Box Full of Letters

IT IS WIDELY ACKNOWLEDGED that the infantry battles in northwestern Europe during World War II were fought by very young men. As Paul Fussell notes in *The Boys' Crusade,* "The European ground war in the west was largely fought by American boys seventeen, eighteen, and nineteen years old. At seventeen you could enlist if you had your parents' written permission, but most boys waited until they were drafted at age eighteen. . . . These infantry soldiers, if they weren't children, weren't quite men either."[1] The youth of troops during the final years of the war is not surprising, given that increasing numbers of soldiers were needed to fight as the war expanded on both the Pacific and the European fronts. Over sixteen million armed forces personnel served in World War II, and infantry soldiers serving in Europe during the battles after D-Day were especially likely to be young, though their youth may have been one of the few things they had in common. These "boy soldiers" of the late battles of the European theater were conscripted (or enlisted) after high school graduation or perhaps a semester of college. They were introduced to M1 rifles, C rations, and bivouacs at camps around the United States. They were delivered to the shores of England or France on crowded troopships. They were thrown into battle with as little as seventeen weeks' training. They watched their buddies die, learned to both respect and resent their superior officers, and came to see the world and some of its people in ways they had never imagined. And all this before they were allowed to drink legally, or to vote for the leaders who were sending them into war.

Most of these boys entered the war with great idealism. Robert Kotlowitz writes in his memoir *Before Their Time,*

> *I believed in the war. It seemed just and righteous to me. In my simpleminded adolescent way, I hated the Nazis. I knew that terrible things were happening everywhere. I understood perfectly well . . . that I was living in a murderous century, one without pity and probably without precedent.*
>
> *I was ready to go.*[2]

Indeed, these boys as a group had all the common accoutrements of late adolescence. They had great energy, which served them well on their twenty-mile hikes during basic training and the difficult marches through the backwoods of France, Belgium, and Germany. They had a sense of being part of something big and important. They had a desire to go beyond the lives of their parents and beyond the borders of their childhood stomping grounds. And—at least initially—they had a belief in their nation's morality and their personal immortality. "Taken as a whole, the boys had a powerful propulsion of optimism, a sense that the war couldn't last forever, and that if anyone was going to get wounded, it would not be them."[3]

Most of the boys who enlisted or were drafted into the military during this time served overseas, and almost three-quarters of them were stationed abroad for an average of sixteen months. Nearly 300,000 U.S. soldiers were killed in battle, and another 114,000 died off the battlefield.[4] The remainder of the soldiers came back home; 671,000 of these returning veterans were injured, and undoubtedly all were changed.

The time between the ages of eighteen and twenty-two is one of maturation and transformation for all young adults. The pursuits of childhood and adolescence—playing, learning, acting in the role of a son or daughter—shift as an individual takes on the responsibilities of adulthood. Marriage, higher education, parenthood, employment: all these markers of adulthood are typically taken on between eighteen and twenty-two. For the "boys" entering World War II and growing into adulthood during this period, however, the transformation was distinctive in several ways.

First, these boys were born during the 1920s and grew up in the midst of the Great Depression. Though the level and nature of hardship they experienced varied substantially depending on where they lived (for instance, in rural as opposed to urban areas) and on their parents' employment, most children felt the effects of the Depression on their family lives and felt at least some degree of economic insecurity and uncertainty about the future. "For many," as Glen Elder notes, "the armed forces in World War II offered a release from a deprived family situation. . . . Service also offered a timeout for men who were unsure of the course to follow in life, though it was a timeout they might not survive."[5] Second, given the effect of economic conditions on mobility at this point in U.S. history, most of these boys had been insulated within their own particular way of life, so military service offered them a chance to see the world through different eyes. As one veteran observed after the war, "When I was in the service, I found myself living among fellows from all over the country. . . . When you talk . . . with them and get their slant on things, it sort of opens up your horizons . . . You start thinking in broader terms than you did before."[6]

Finally, entering the military at a young age could either speed up maturation by providing new and often stressful experiences, or delay it by putting marriage, higher education, and permanent employment—the signposts of growing up—on hold. Glen Elder's study of the life course of World War II veterans found that those who entered the military before twenty-one were most likely to experience a positive redirection of life course as a result of their service. There are several possible explanations for this finding. First, for these young men, service came just after high school, at a natural break between youth and adulthood. Thus, there was less likelihood of its disrupting established patterns such as those inherent in marriage, parenthood, or an established job or career. Further, upon return from the military, these young veterans were able to take full advantage of the GI Bill and other benefits for education, housing, and employment that were afforded to returning soldiers, improving their chances for educational and economic success later in life.[7]

The experience of war—and especially of combat—by its nature has profound effects, both positive and negative. The negative ones include combat anxieties, life disruption, economic ills, separation from loved ones, and concerns about death and destruction. The positive effects include learning to cope with adversity, and developing greater self-discipline, a clearer sense of direction, a broader perspective, and enhanced job skills.[8] For both better and worse, then, the experience of war and combat is transformative. The men who returned from Europe in late 1945 and early 1946 were not the boys who had entered the war several years earlier.

One of Those Boys

My father, Joe Ted Miller, was one of these boys transformed into men. He was born November 14, 1925, in rural Illinois. He was a smart student, the valedictorian of his high school class. He was drafted during his first semester at the University of Illinois and began his training at Camp Blanding, Florida, in January 1944. He was trained in code and as a radio operator at Camp Blanding and was transferred to Camp Van Dorn, Mississippi, in June 1944. He continued his training there, then shipped out from New York on November 25,

1944, and landed in Marseilles on December 8. As he noted in the heading to one of his letters home, during his battle time in France and Germany he was "with the Radio Section of the Communications Platoon of the Second Battalion of the 254th Regiment of the 63rd Infantry division of the 21st Corps of the Seventh Army of the European Theater of the U.S. Army."[9] His unit earned a Presidential Unit Citation for their role in fighting at the Colmar Pocket, and my father earned a Bronze Star for his work in his unit's push through the Siegfried line. After hostilities ended in Europe, he didn't have the requisite "points" to return stateside, so he stayed in Europe, stationed first in Paris and Versailles and then in Höchst, Germany. He finally shipped back to the United States aboard the SS Ernie Pyle in late March 1946. He was twenty years old.

After he returned to the States, my father reenrolled in the University of Illinois, finishing his degree in three years with the help of the GI Bill. He was successful in college, and he is among the exemplary scholars whose names are inscribed on bronze tablets hanging in the University of Illinois library. But my father's life as a college student was not carefree, for he was also contributing substantially to the support of his mother and his younger sister. His own father had died in June of 1945 while Dad was in Europe, and he was now the "man of the house." He continued to help support his mother as he launched his journalism career with early jobs in San Antonio and New Orleans. He spent the majority of his career on the editorial staff of the *Detroit Free Press.* It was in Detroit that he met my mother (a journalist who worked for the Associated Press during and after the war), and they raised a family of four daughters in the suburbs. I am the third of those daughters.

My father died on March 6, 2006. He had been ill for a number of years with diabetes and had experienced two strokes in 2001. At the end of his life, he was bedbound, incontinent, and suffering from the early stages of dementia. In short, he was ready for the massive heart attack that struck in early March. In his last few months, spent in a nursing home, the caregivers asked him what his job had been before he retired. In spite of his long and highly successful career in the newspaper business, his only answer to this question was, "I was in the Army." This is an interesting response for a man who rarely wanted to talk about his army experiences, who didn't keep up with any of his army buddies, who never participated in organizations like the American Legion or the VFW, and who was generally cynical about all things related to military life.

In going through his effects after his death, my mother and sisters and I came upon a box full of the letters Dad wrote home from the army. The letters began with salutations such as "Dear Mom and Dad" and "Dear Folks" and "Dear Mom and Folks." Many ended with a vertically arranged closing:

Bye
Love
Bud

I had always known these letters existed, but I had been unaware of the sheer number of them or of the breadth of experience they communicated. My sisters and I sat on the floor and read from these letters, marveling at what our father had gone through in the war, reveling in this sudden view of him as a teenager and a young man, and regretting that we hadn't spent more time talking with him about his experiences when he was alive. My sisters and mother were excited when I told them later that I wanted to write about and from these letters, and they promised to support me in the process.

This book, then, is a consideration of one soldier's journey from boy to man during basic training, the final European battles of World War II, and the immediate postwar period in France and Germany. My father grew up in many ways during this time, and I will be examining various aspects of the transformation of his beliefs about fatherhood and family, friendships and relationships, work and bureaucracy, and the larger questions of war and morality. The centerpiece of my analysis is the letters my father wrote to his parents during his stateside training and his time in the European theater of operations and postwar Europe. I will supplement his descriptions of his own experiences with additional accounts of his regiment and division and of the larger war effort. And I will bring to this study social, psychological, and historical research that has focused on not only typical processes of growth and development, but also the ways, both profound and mundane, in which the experience of war can alter such processes. Within that context, however, this book is an account of one man's experience, and it is not meant to be generalized in a systematic way.

The remainder of this prologue will discuss the corpus of materials I have drawn on throughout the book, my position in analyzing the material, and the content and structure of coming chapters.

Sources for Analysis

Early in his correspondence, on February 3, 1944, my father writes to his parents, "Like you suggested, Mom, I've decided to keep a diary—but in a different way. I'll write you a letter each night, if possible, and then you can save the letters—that is, if you want to do so." Over the next twenty-five months, my father kept this promise. He didn't write every day—especially once in Europe and engaged in battle—but he wrote very regularly. And although I don't know whether my grandmother saved all of his letters, I do know that 318 of them survived to be found in that box over sixty years later. These include 178 letters written during stateside training and 140 from Europe. The early stateside epistles are handwritten on stationery provided by my grandfather's small print shop and embossed with my father's name and "U.S. Army." The letters from Europe are on whatever paper could be found—usually plain copy paper or onionskin, but occasionally letterhead from the USO or Red Cross, or "found" stationery from a French or German home. These letters from Europe are sometimes handwritten but more often typed, as my father worked in the communications section of his unit and often had ready access to typewriters. Some letters are single pages, but most are multiple pages.

My father's correspondence reflects on many aspects of his life in the military. In the letters, Dad frequently discusses food (both the C rations and the good meals), things he bought at the PX, and movies he saw during off-hours. Many letters provide both general and specific requests for packages from home. The letters provide short biographies of friends and platoon-mates, discussions of training activities, and complaints about (and occasionally a bit of admiration for) officers. There is some discussion of actual battle experiences, but this type of content is limited and circumspect (perhaps by choice, likely by the prospect of censors). When he is moving or on leave, my father provides travelogues of what he sees. His letters are replete with yearnings for home and affection for "the best darn people around." Dad occasionally waxes philosophic as he writes, sharing ideas about the war effort, bureaucracy, cultural differences, and the meaning of life. His journalistic leanings are clear from the objective detail with which he often reports on his experiences, but his feelings are far from hidden as he expresses frustration with army life, a mix of fear at the dangers of being where he is and gratitude that he isn't at the very front line, and homesickness for his family and all things American. Indeed, it is clear from these letters that the value of Pepsi-Cola could not be overestimated for the GIs.

Although the letters from my father to his parents (and later to just his mother) are central to the description and analysis in this book, the texts and narratives of the letters are, as noted above, supplemented by—and indeed seen through the prism of—several additional sources of information.

First, I draw extensively on additional family archives and on personal archives that my father kept from his time in the war. The family archives include a genealogy of the Miller family, my father's high school yearbook, family photos, newspaper clippings, and correspondence between my father and his daughters during our childhood and later in our lives. I also draw extensively on a 56-page personal memoir of childhood written by my father in the late 1980s and make some use of a 191-page novel in manuscript form that he wrote in 1988, as well as other notes made after his retirement. I have supplemented these written family archives with an interview with my father's sister, Judith Parsons, shortly before her death in 2007, and with ongoing discussions with my mother and my sisters. In the category of personal archives from the war years, I draw information and insight from a small diary that my father kept in 1945, photos of his war buddies, official military paperwork, and a complete list of his locations during his time in Europe. He kept that list in his role as clerk in the headquarters company of his infantry battalion.

Second, I have drawn extensively on materials relevant to my father's specific experiences in the military with the 63rd Infantry Division (254th Regiment). I have considered written materials including a 1945 "official" unit history, *The Trail of the 254th thru Blood & Fire* by Harris Peel and colleagues, a 1945 division booklet titled *Victory in Europe,* and a 1986 book by Col. James E. Hatcher, *With the 63rd Infantry Division in WWII.* Through helpful contact with the 63rd Infantry Association, I have also been able to draw on CD archives of materials including copies of the *Blood and Fire* newspapers, the 63rd Infantry Division chronicles, pictorial histories of both the 254th Regiment and the 63rd Infantry Division, and maps detailing locations and activities of the division during its time in Europe. I have in addition relied on remembrances of other members of the 63rd in the *Blood and Fire* newsletter, still published by the infantry association, and I was able to interview one of my father's war buddies, Carl Brass, in the summer of 2009. Finally, I was afforded insight through a visit to the Camp Blanding Museum near Jacksonville, Florida, and from the website commemorating the now-defunct Camp Van Dorn in Mississippi.

In making sense of these materials, I have relied substantially on two areas of published literature. The first of these is the extensive body of work about combat and noncombat experiences during World War II, especially in the European theater. These sources include historical treatments as well as memoirs and oral histories. In conjunction with this body of scholarship, I have also looked at the more limited work on the experience of childhood in the Great Depression. Second, particularly in the chapters of this book that look more analytically at my father's transition from boy to man, I have relied on published theoretical and empirical work relevant to that transition. Writing in this area includes, in addition to general treatments of the maturation process, considerations of masculinity, studies on the development and maintenance of friendship, research on work socialization, discussions of moral development, and specific studies of the effects of war and combat on those who serve in the military.

My Analytical Position

The descriptions, reflections, and analysis in the coming chapters sit at the crossroads of several traditions within scholarship and writing. For example, there is a long tradition of analyzing correspondence, and recent years have brought particular interest to the letters written by soldiers during World War II.[10] Many of the materials, however, are simple compilations of letters with limited commentary, or letters put together by the soldier to create a narrative account of his own experiences.[11] Similarly, oral histories such as Studs Terkel's *"The Good War"*[12] provide an understanding of the experience of particular soldiers in their own words, but largely let the words speak for themselves, with limited additional analysis. On the other end of the spectrum are scholarly books that analyze specific issues, such as the development of masculinity in historical context.[13] Another such issue is the formulation of adult identity.[14] To this mix can be added scholarly biographies, the personal memoirs of the famous and not-so-famous, and histories based on meticulous examination of primary sources. The present work borrows from many of these traditions, but is not clearly situated in any of them. Thus, it is important to consider my own position in the process of description, analysis, and writing.

This book can perhaps be best described as an "interpretive biography," which Norman Denzin defines as "the studied use and collection of personal-life documents, stories, accounts, and narratives which describe turning-point moments in individuals' lives."[15] Denzin argues that interpretive biographical (and autobiographical) work—especially within the larger tradition of sociology—can be distinguished from traditional biography in its emphasis on sociological and event-based analysis. Further, interpretive biography is marked by several concepts or conventions that serve as frames for the work. "These conventions," Denzin writes, "which structure how lives are told and written about, involve the following problematic presuppositions, and taken-for-granted assumptions: (1) the existence of others, (2) the influence and importance of gender and class, (3) family beginnings, (4) starting points, (5) known and knowing authors and observers, (6) objective life markers,

(7) real persons with real lives, (8) turning-point experiences, (9) truthful statements distinguished from fictions."[16]

War Makes Men of Boys will involve all these conventions of interpretive biography. What might be seen, however, as particularly problematic is being a "knowing author" with a personal understanding of the subject's life, and distinguishing truthful statements from fictions. I have had to confront both these issues in my multiple positions as daughter, analyst, and author.

Because I am writing about my father, I am clearly not an "objective" investigator in the scientific sense of this term, and I cannot look at these materials with the distanced and analytical eye of a rhetorical critic, a historian, or a scholarly biographer. Though I never knew the teenager and young man who wrote these letters, I do know the man and father he became, and my view of the materials is colored by that knowledge. Such closeness of author to subject matter is less uncommon than it used to be; in recent years, several scholars in the communication discipline have written about their families. Among them is Nick Trujillo, who has examined the meaning of his grandmother's life through correspondence, family artifacts, and family interviews.[17] And Bud Goodall explored his experiences growing up in a family immersed in and influenced by (though not necessarily knowing it) the clandestine practices of the CIA.[18]

In both of these projects, the authors' thoughts and feelings are intimately and intricately woven into both the analysis and the narrative. My project is similar to these in that I am an academic who, in examining a portion of my family's history, must be alert to the ways in which my role as a daughter influences my role as a scholar. Further, my personal understandings of the man my father became are essential aspects of the project. But I will attempt to keep the focus clearly on my father's experiences and relationships. I am interested in understanding those experiences within the context of history, family, relationships, and society. I am also interested in using this admittedly singular interpretive biography to develop insights into broader questions of how young people navigate complicated turning points thrown at them by external events and internal struggles as they move from childhood to adulthood.

The Chapters Ahead

The chapters ahead, then, are a journey through twenty-six months of my father's life at a formative age, at a critical moment in history, and in places far away from his home. But these chapters will also attempt to link his experiences during the war to some of his experiences later in life and to larger discourses about family, friendship, relationships, masculinity, work, war, and morality. The first two chapters are the longest of the book and take on the descriptive portion of this task. In them, my emphasis is on creating full descriptions of my father's boyhood and his army life that are faithful to his letters, his other writings, and other accounts of the time. In chapter 1, "Bud Joins the Army," I take up my father's childhood in a poor family in rural Illinois and then follow his experiences during the first eleven months of his military service while he was in basic training in Florida and Mississippi. In chapter 2, "Bud Goes to War," I follow him first from Camp Van Dorn in Mississippi as he ships out to Europe, then through the European theater in the last five months of combat, and finally through his time in postwar Europe in France and Germany. I have attempted to contextualize the description of my father's wartime experiences by considering them within the larger European narrative.

In the next four chapters, I adopt a more analytical frame as I consider my father's transition from boy to man across several aspects of life development. In chapter 3, "Family and Fatherhood," I look at his shifting ideas about family—and his shifting role within his family—over his twenty-six months in the service. My grandfather's death in June 1945 is a turning point from which I analyze changes in my father's beliefs about fatherhood and family. In chapter 4, "Buddies and Girlfriends," I consider the ways in which his attitudes about friendship and relationships changed through his experiences with a variety of people both in the army and on the home front. In chapter 5, "Work and Bureaucracy," I examine the ways in which his shifting ideas about work, career, and organizations—paradoxical ideas that included both idealism and cynicism—were shaped by his observations of self and others within the army system. Finally, in chapter 6, "Public and Private Morality," I explore the development of my father's beliefs about moral behavior on both the individual level and the larger world stage. In these four analytical chapters, through a close textual analysis of his writing informed by theoretical understandings of personality, relationships, family development, work, and morality, I try to understand the changes my father underwent. The book closes with an epilogue, "A Reluctant Member of the Greatest Generation," that assesses my father's experiences—and the development of his life in light of those experiences—within the context of contemporary commentary about the World War II generation.

CHAPTER ONE

Bud Joins the Army

THROUGHOUT HIS LIFE, my father disliked his name. In his later-life writings about the "good things" and "bad things" that happened during childhood, he notes that the first good thing was being born, and the first bad one was being named. Though in searching through Army records I found that he was known as Joseph T. Miller by parts of the military bureaucracy, his given name was Joe Ted. In official family lore, the "Joe" part was in honor of Joe Cannon, a powerful politician from Danville, Illinois, who served as speaker of the U.S. House of Representatives from 1903 to 1911, and the "Ted" part was for Teddy Roosevelt, whom my father's father also greatly admired. Interestingly, these two namesakes were known for their political clashes, and each of them actually bore the longer moniker of Joseph or Theodore. The unofficial backstory of my father's name is that my grandmother disliked nicknames, so she used them—"Joe" and "Ted"—for the given names of her only son. However, throughout his childhood, my father was called "Bud" or "Buddy"—"Joe Ted" was used even by his nickname-hating mother only when disciplinary action was in order. As my father asks in his memoir, "What kind of logic is that?" A mother's logic, apparently, but it stuck. Dad's army letters were all signed "Bud."

Bud as a Child

My father was born November 14, 1925, in Danville, Illinois, a mid-sized town near the Indiana border east of the college town of Urbana and its sister city, Champaign. He was the middle child and only son of Oscar Francis and Irene Miller. His sister Dorothy was ten years old when he was born, and his younger sister, Judith, was born in 1931. He lived in Danville through the third grade, in a series of houses of which he remembered little. Dorothy told him later that "each one was worse than the one before, as the Depression struck and the money trickled away" (quoted in the memoir). In the summer of 1934, Dad's father lost his printing job and had to search for a new one. My father writes in his memoir that "Dad started hitchhiking west, stopping in Champaign and Urbana and in each little town—Fithian, St. Joe, Gibson City, Monticello—to ask about printshop jobs. It must have taken a lot of courage for him to do this. But then, in those times courage was born out of desperation. When you can't feed your family, you will do nearly anything." Oscar finally found employment in Bement, a small farming community sixty miles west of Danville. The family's first house in Bement had running water and electricity, but no indoor plumbing. Dad recalls that "it sure was cold, trotting out to the outhouse in the dead of winter. It made one strive to hold back the urges."

Three years later, after Dad had completed sixth grade, a new and better job at a print shop in Champaign led to another move for the family. Dad attended Junior High in Champaign; then the family moved across town to Urbana, after Oscar had accumulated enough money to start his own shop. The store, Dad remembers, "was in the rear and we had living quarters in the front, curtained off from the shop. There was not nearly the room we had had in Champaign, and I imagine Mom was distraught about the whole thing. But Dad had the start of his dream. It lasted only five years and never was a success. When he died he owed money to various people, including the postman. Mom went to work to pay off the debts, and gave the postman our gas kitchen stove for the interest."

My father and his family continued to live in Urbana, and he graduated from Urbana High School in 1943, one of several valedictorians. He was awarded a county scholarship to attend the University of Illinois and enrolled in classes for the summer after his senior year in high school. But that fall he turned eighteen and was quickly drafted. He left for his induction center at Fort Sheridan in northeastern Illinois in January 1944.

Many aspects of my father's childhood were typical of countless rural or small-town childhoods during the Great Depression. Both his grandfathers were deep-hole coal miners in the mines of southern Illinois, and my father's parents clearly remembered the poverty of their own youth and wanted better things for themselves and their children. Work was hard to come by in those years, and my grandfather struggled to find employment and to keep his family afloat. When my father was in the fifth grade and his mother contracted pneumonia, there was no money to pay the hospital for her care. This undoubtedly rankled the proud family. My father's younger sister, Judy, had to sleep on a cot in a hallway until she was almost a teenager. There were apparently many arguments about money, especially when my grandfather's ambition for his own print shop butted up against my grandmother's goal of basic economic security. "It seemed she was almost blaming Dad for the whole Depression even though he was doing his best to make a go of his work. I think she was afraid of his consuming desire to own his own shop, and would have preferred that he try to get a better job and draw a regular paycheck."

But the Miller family managed throughout the long Depression, though perhaps not in the best of living situations or with a great many luxuries. Luckily, the luxuries probably didn't matter much to young children. "We were always 'dirt poor,' as my mother said," Dad wrote, "but never poverty-stricken to the extent that we were starving. And somehow, my Dad and Mom could scare up an occasional dime for a soda and did what they could to make it a happy life."

Many years later, my father remembered details of everyday life in his Depression-era family. Some of his memories suggest how the family economized in small ways. He remembers that though his father loved bacon, they would often get "side meat" (salt pork) instead because it was cheaper, and that when low-priced margarine was introduced to stores, it came with an envelope of orange powder that could be worked into the lard-like substance to give it a buttery appearance. The family raised chickens in the backyard: "Mom would kill the chicken by grabbing it, holding a broomstick on its neck and twisting its head off. She was very quick and good at it." Soft-drink choice was dictated by economics, as well: "Dad loved Coke but when Pepsi came out with its 'twice as much for a nickel, too,' he switched over." Dad also recalled pastimes of the era, with both friends ("We used the knives to play mumble-peg at recess in the fall and spring. I was mediocre at the game and often had to pay the penalty, which was pulling a matchstick out of the ground with my teeth") and family ("My Dad played the bones—dried out beef rib bones which you shook between your fingers to get a rhythmic clattering sound"). Many of his writings recall details of everyday life that seem very foreign decades later, such as stopping an interurban train by lighting a match and throwing it on the track, or going to the door every morning to pick up the Meadow Gold milk with its "frozen cream which popped up from the neck."

Several threads that run through my father's childhood reminiscences define important aspects of his growing-up years. The first of these is education. My father's parents never completed high school, yet they were clearly intelligent and they had great respect for education. In the early years, my father admired teachers who taught the old-fashioned way, by emphasizing rote learning and disciplining poor behavior with corporal punishment. Dad clearly viewed this kind of education—both the memorization and the paddling—as a good thing. "I think my teachers in Bement—all women—did a great job of giving their kids a good basic grade school education. Nobody ever was punished for failure to learn, however. There was a little homework, and if you didn't do it, you did get punished. But the teachers helped you learn and didn't blame you if you had trouble with it." Past elementary school, my father continued his good academic performance and was rewarded for it. He was the county representative for a state spelling bee broadcast on the radio. He made excellent grades in all his subjects. He participated in the state Latin contest in high school, although he lamented that those private-school kids from Chicago were tough to beat. And he graduated from high school at the top of his class and won a scholarship to the University of Illinois.

A second part of his childhood that was clearly important to my father was hunting and fishing. The hunting was mostly for very small game—squirrels, rabbits, even pigeons. "It was so pleasant to sit under a tree with Dad in those woods and wait for a squirrel to poke its head out. I never felt sorry for the squirrels that we shot. They made delicious eating." One of my father's most valued Christmas presents was a single-shot .22 rifle. Fishing was even dearer to his heart than hunting. With his father, sisters, and family friends, he fished mostly on the Vermilion River. For a few years, the fishing parties stayed in a one-room cabin that Oscar built on a distant relative's property. "We caught mostly carp and catfish, although a little ways from the Cabin was a sandbar where the water ran a little swifter and where there were a few bass." The best spot for fishing, though, was at Rocky Ford, on the Salt Fork of the Vermilion River. The bass fishing was good there, and my father was excited to try out his "Pfleuger tandem spinner," a newfangled artificial lure. He notes, though, that "Dad was more practical. . . . He'd turn over a few rocks in those shallow eddies, find some helgramites (black wormlike creatures with fierce pincers) or crawfish (which pinched but not so severely). He'd pop the helgramites and crawfish into his straw hat and then put his hat on. Apparently the critters didn't bother to pinch his mostly bald head, or else he just ignored them. He said it was the easiest way to carry bait."

And sports were also of great importance to my father during childhood. There was some actual playing of sports (neighborhood games of "round-ball," and running track a bit in junior high), but my father was small and not particularly athletic. He was, however, a great follower of sports at all levels. He and his father were both Chicago Cubs fans, and he clearly remembered his only trip to Wrigley Field as a child and an earlier trip to St. Louis to see the Cubs play the Cardinals at Sportsman's Park. He listened at night to the

Chicago Black Hawks on a small radio under his pillow, though his mother got angry at him for staying awake past his bedtime. As an eighth grader, he became a "stringer" for the local newspaper, calling in scores for all the junior high games, and he continued his work as a sports writer for the *News-Gazette* in high school and college. He wrote with great fondness of going to University of Illinois football games. "I'd take a bus to the stadium and get a student seat in the end zone for 40 cents. Illinois didn't have a good team, so it was a great thrill when the Illini beat Michigan in 1939, when I was in the ninth grade." After that game he wrote a poem about it entitled "What a Game"; it opened with these stanzas:

It was November the fourth in '39,
That the Illinois team felt mighty fine,
They felt so good that they beat Michigan,
The team with Harmon, the mighty man.

Tom was heralded like Grange, the great,
But little did he know his fate,
For the fighting Illini blocked his passes,
They made the Wolverines look like asses.

One of my father's fondest youthful memories of sports was attending the Illinois state high school basketball tournament the year he was in ninth grade. He won a lottery for the tickets ($3.50 for the entire tournament) and wrote of the experience, "Eight games—two in the morning, three in the afternoon, and three in the evening—were held on the first day of the tournament, Thursday. There was a huge map of Illinois at one end of the gym, with lights for the 16 teams involved. When a team was eliminated its light went out. I considered it a marvelous day, watching the games amid all the excitement. I loved the LaGrange team because of the cheerleaders, the prettiest I had ever seen."

Finally, throughout my father's memoir about his childhood is the sense of a loving family and of his enduring affection for his mother, father, and sisters. My father saw his mother as the parent with great ambitions for him and with the disciplinary bent to make those ambitions a reality. "Mom was determined that her son was going to do the right things and do them well, and she used her strap to emphasize her determination." But he never doubted that she was motivated by a deep and abiding love. His relationship with his father was close, too; it was based on the love of shared activities. Together they fished and hunted, reveled in the successes of their favorite sports teams (like Gabby Hartnett's "homer in the gloaming" for the Cubs in 1938), listened to *Amos and Andy* and *Fibber McGee and Molly* on the radio, and occasionally attended a cowboy movie at the local cinema. Dad especially loved the times he could go back to the printshop at night with his father. "Mom never let me go on school nights, but on Saturday nights I'd sometimes go back with him, to fool around at setting type or to write on scratch paper or to run the job press slowly. We'd trade puns a lot. Dad loved puns. One time he told me, 'Did Miss-ouri wear the New Jersey or did Miss-issippi?' and then answered himself, 'Idaho.'"

Addressing young readers in a photography book about the Great Depression, Russell Freedman writes that it "widened the gap between America's haves and have-nots. Many children and teenagers belonged to families that were comfortably well off and were not badly hurt by the economic crisis. But millions of kids grew up poor. Some children lived under conditions we associate today with impoverished developing nations. They could only dream of a world in which childhood is a time of innocence and play."[1] My father's memories of his childhood, however, suggest that there was clearly some "in-between" in this dichotomy, particularly for children. His father struggled to stay employed, and the family was uprooted on several occasions as he looked for work. Paying bills was a constant challenge, and side meat instead of bacon, Pepsi instead of Coke, an outhouse instead of plumbing, and inability to pay hospital bills were not the only inconveniences the family suffered. But in spite of the significant stress caused by financial privation, and in spite of the frequent arguments that broke out about it between his parents, for my father, childhood was happy.

It was largely a time of learning and of play. His mother may have described the family as "dirt poor," but my father always had a roof over his head and food to eat. He remained in school and was not forced to work to help support his family, and he was by and large protected from the domestic problems brought on by hard times. He not only fished and hunted with his father, but played with neighborhood friends, listened to the radio, and enjoyed occasional outings to the movie theater and sporting events. My father had many fond memories of his childhood, and he concluded his memoir by asserting with conviction that "growing up poor certainly did not mean growing up unhappy."

But when the Japanese bombed Pearl Harbor less than a month after my father's sixteenth birthday, he must have realized that his future might not be quite what he had envisioned for himself during childhood. On December 20,

1941, the draft was extended to men between the ages of twenty and forty-five, and on November 13, 1942 (the day before his seventeenth birthday), the draft age was lowered to eighteen. Dad might have been hoping for a place in the Army Specialized Training Program (ASTP), a merit-based program created by a special act of Congress and designed to train officers. It was open to enlistees from eighteen to twenty-two who had high school diplomas and who tested high on IQ.[2] In the middle part of 1943, about 150,000 soldiers were assigned to ASTP units at over two hundred colleges and universities, and my father would probably have qualified for this program. But the program didn't last, and by early in 1944, these "best and brightest" were being assigned to infantry replacement training camps. My father didn't have a chance to be disappointed by this shift in policy, though, as the ASTP stopped accepting recruits shortly before his eighteenth birthday. So when that birthday arrived in November 1943, he joined thousands of other young men as a regular draftee in the U.S. Army.

Bud in Basic Training

> These people, they really put you in your place. That's a polite way of sayin' it. They humiliate ya, they make ya do things that you don't think are physically possible. At the same time, they're makin' you feel you're something. That you're part of something. When you're there and you need somebody, you got somebody.
>
> ROGER TUTTRUP, IN STUDS TERKEL'S *The Good War*

Military training is all about the transformation from civilian to soldier—the "process by which light-hearted college boys are made into battle-ready warriors."[3] My father did the first major portion of his training at Camp Blanding, an infantry replacement training center near Jacksonville, Florida, that was established early in the U.S. war effort. Presumably, when Dad arrived at Camp Blanding, he received the "*IRTC Handbook—Camp Blanding, Florida,*" a small booklet that laid out expectations for trainees and provided information about the camp and surrounding area. The handbook began with a clear statement regarding the dire need for new inductees to make the transformation from civilian to soldier:

> *You are here as a trainee because your country is engaged in a life and death struggle with one of the most powerful and ruthless combinations of powers*

> *the world has ever known. Our enemies are tough, cruel and highly trained. Their defeat is essential before this world can become a decent place in which to live. The defeat of the enemy cannot be accomplished by amateurs or half-trained men. During the seventeen weeks intensive training you will find the work hard, the hours long, the going tough in spots, as it should be. If, however, you concentrate your energy and determination on your work you will become an alert, confident, skilled soldier, prepared to function as a member of a combat division.*[4]

This transformation from civilian to fighting soldier involved many dimensions. The civilian had to learn to dress and talk and act like a soldier. He had to be physically toughened to endure battle as a soldier. He had to learn to fire (and clean) a rifle, throw a hand grenade, use a gas mask, and survive for days in grueling outdoor conditions. Often he had to learn specialized and highly technical tasks for particular army units. At the most basic level, the inductee had to shed the identity of civilian—the comforts of family and everyday life—and take on the mind-set and attitudes of the military.

For my father, this transformation began in late January 1944. Before he had a chance to read the inspirational rhetoric of the Camp Blanding IRTC Handbook, he had to part from his family and go through the process of military induction. His first postcard home was written on Wednesday, January 26, just hours after he arrived at Fort Sheridan, one of four national recruit reception centers. Inductees from throughout the Midwest were funneled through Fort Sheridan on their way to basic training at military bases around the country. My father was there for only three days, but that was enough time for his transformation from civilian to soldier to begin in earnest. His two letters from Fort Sheridan report on his regimented schedule, his bunk in the barracks, food that is "O.K.—not home-cooked, though," the inoculation shots he received, his new GI haircut, and the tests he had to take: "mechanical aptitude (I did terrible), radio (easier) and IQ (not enough time)." He also starts picking up bits of soldier lingo, and his last letter from Fort Sheridan, on January 29, 1944, opens with, "I've been 'bingoed.' That means I'm being shipped, along with some other of the boys." He tells his folks, "Have to wear regulation O.D.'s (Olive Drab) out, along with our helmets." He then boarded the train and left for the first major phase of his life in the army.

In a letter headed "Enroute to God-only-knows-where (Jan. 29–Feb. 1)," Dad reports that at 2:45 p.m. on Saturday, January 29, there was an "assembly of 320 assorted characters for shipping." The train left more than two hours later and finally got through Chicago at 9:00 p.m. For the next two days the recruits moved through the country, and my father provided a travelogue in the form of a long letter. At 10:00 a.m. on Sunday, the train crossed the "very foggy Ohio River" with the "Mississippi River rolling along on our right." He reports that Kentucky is "woods, rolling hills, and small dirty towns. Seems to be good squirrel country, Dad." He reports much of the same for Tennessee, although he notes an increasing number of cotton fields and lots of red, brown, and yellow clay—different from the "good black land" of Illinois. At 1:00 p.m. on Sunday, they rolled through Jackson, Tennessee. "Quite a town—shacks—negroes—barefoot kids—people in shirt sleeves—boys playing baseball. Hotter & hotter." Seven hours later, the train passed through Birmingham, Alabama. "Good sized city—about 200,000. Can see red glow of steel mills all around us. Boys currently whistling at girls out the windows." By 3:00 p.m. on Monday, they had crossed into Florida. He reports on the "vegetation and swampy land" of the Everglades and adds, "Everyone on the train now agrees we are headed for Camp Blanding, near Jacksonville. . . . We are in the infantry."

This news was probably not a great surprise to my father and the other recruits on the train. Most of soldiers serving in the army during World War II were in the infantry—they were foot soldiers who fought at the front lines, as foot soldiers have done throughout history. The role of the infantry in World War II was critically important and incredibly hard. Ernie Pyle said, "I love the infantry because they are the underdogs. They are the mud-rain-frost-and-wind boys. They have no comforts, and they even learn to live without the necessities. And in the end they are the guys that wars can't be won without."[5] British Field Marshal Earl Wavell was equally direct about the centrality of the infantryman in war and the difficulty and dangers of his job: "Let us be clear about three facts," he said. "First, all battles and all wars are won in the end by the infantryman. Secondly, the infantryman always bears the brunt. His casualties are heavier, he suffers greater extremes of discomfort and fatigue than the other arms. Thirdly, the art of the infantryman is less stereotyped and far harder to acquire in modern war than that of any other arm."[6]

The boys on the train arriving at Camp Blanding must have known that as future infantrymen they were in for a test of their physical, mental, and emotional strength. Their success at the complex weapons training could mean the difference between life and death. Further, they must have known that the dangers for new infantrymen at this point in the war were especially pronounced. Over the course of the war, the infantry suffered 627,521 casualties, many more than any other military branch.[7] So when my father says later in his letter, after talking about the possibility of specialized training, that "all of us are definitely in the infantry whether we go to a school or not," he is acknowledging a move into a difficult and perilous future.

My father probably saw the news about being stationed at Camp Blanding for the coming weeks in a relatively positive light (he notes at the end of his travelogue letter that "this is a pretty fair camp"). Camp Blanding had been established in 1939 as a training reservation for the Florida National Guard. As the prospect of U.S. involvement in World War II increased, however, the camp was converted into a federal reservation at which hundreds of thousands of troops were trained, including cavalry, tank destroyer, field artillery, engineering, medical, and other specialized personnel. As the *Camp Blanding Handbook* points out, "Camp Blanding mushroomed from an entirely undeveloped wasteland into a tremendous military reservation spanning over 125,000 acres—the fourth largest city in the State of Florida."[8] This large camp included seven movie theaters, twenty-five PXs, multiple service clubs and dayrooms, and an expansive swimming facility on Lake Kingsley. In 1943 the camp was established as Camp Blanding Infantry Replacement Training Center (IRTC), and nine entire infantry divisions were trained there. My father's division was the 63rd, officially activated in June 1943. It was the "Blood and Fire" division, so named from Winston Churchill's vow at the Casablanca Conference in early 1943 to make the enemies of the Allies "bleed and burn in expiation of their crimes against humanity."

My father was stationed at Camp Blanding from February 1, 1944, until the second week of June 1944. At the end of that short eighteen-week period, he was no longer just a teenager months out of high school. He had become a soldier trained to fight for the U.S. Army. Basic training—at its core—serves the fundamental task of turning civilians into soldiers. Young men coming into Camp Blanding during World War II had to learn to talk like soldiers, act like soldiers, and understand the basics of military life. Most of the details of life at camp and rules about dress, schedules, transportation, pay, recreation, medical care, and assorted aspects of protocol were outlined in the *IRTC Handbook* that recruits received on arrival. The recruits were also quickly exposed to classes that provided them with context regarding the war effort and their place in that effort. Much of their instruction involved the safeguarding of military information, and my father obviously took these lessons seriously. On February 10 he wrote, "Today was another hard day—we didn't get off till 8:30—but I rather enjoyed the work. Inasmuch as (get the big word) we were shown very interesting films on security from 6:30–8:30 tonite, I won't tell you (I can't) much about the camp from now on." A week later the recruits were still watching films about security, and Dad noted that they were "Excellent pictures ('don't talk, the walls have enemy ears, etc., etc.')."

The early days of basic training were also a time of getting used to the various duties to which recruits were assigned. On several occasions Dad wrote letters while on guard duty. On March 9 he says, "I'm in the third relief, on duty 11–1 & 5–7. You can see that's pretty good. 4 solid hours of sleep from 1–5 I'll get. Have to dress in O.D.'s, carry rifles, bayonets, cartridge belts, wear helmets." The duty he talked about most, though, was KP, perhaps because he thought his mother could relate to it ("Well, Mom, I know just how you feel now"). On February 24, he details the army way of working in the kitchen: "After cleaning up this morning after chow (scrub floors, wash dishes, etc.) we (me & 5 others) peeled 25 gallons of potatoes. Then it was dinnertime & more dishwashing, etc. Peeled some more spuds in afternoon. After supper cleaned out stoves, did regular scrubbing, & were then dismissed. You may not believe this, Mom, but we wash the dishes—all of them—for 180 men in about an hour. There is no drying of dishes, just wash, rinse, & set out. It's quite a system."

As he took on a soldier's identity, Dad included terminology in his letters to demonstrate his growing army vocabulary ("I am well stocked with D-rations. Candy bars to you"). He describes the rules for various passes, protocol for interacting with officers of different ranks, and the foodstuffs included in a pack of C rations. Though much of his use of army language was by way of informing his folks, there's often a hint—or more than a hint—of bragging about his new lexicon. In discussing part of his training in radio operations in a letter sent April 12, 1944, he writes: "We set up SCR284's today. They are powerful radios. 25-ft aerial & all. I'll tell you how we set up the SCR284. Take the BC654A, attach the four LG13A's, attach the two LG2A's to the GN45 which comes out of the CS41. Then put the CD501A on the GN45. Put the HS30 on the BC654A. Attach the CP12 & CP13 from the RL29. Put up the MS4956 with IN106A, GY11, GY12, & GPZ7's. Put the BA43 & PE104 in, attach the RM29 & CS76, & the SWCR284 is complete. Understand?"

My father's growing sense of identity as a soldier can also be seen in his humor and in his recounting of typical basic training jokes. His letter of February 10 is headed with the underlined comment, "Secret ambition—to be a Pfc—poor fool civilian," which is followed with "Typical Co. A joke—Girl (after deposit on hat by bird)—Get some paper, quick. Boy—What for, the bird's a mile away by now." And, in spite of his general satisfaction with the facilities at Camp Blanding, on February 20 he shared a joke that was undoubtedly told by recruits at basic training sites across the country:

Jonesy told me this one today:
3 infantrymen killed in N. Africa were seeking admittance to Heaven—
St. Peter—"and where did you have basic training, John Smith?"
Smith—"Fort Orr, Oregon."
St. Peter—"Well, you'll have to wait in line over there."—"and where did you have basic, Henry Jones?"
Jones—"Ft. Meade, Md."
St. Peter—"Well, you'll have to wait in line over there."—"and where did you have basic, Jim Doe?"
Doe—"Camp Blanding, Florida."
St. Peter—"Go right on in—you've been in Hell long enough."

The many changes that my father underwent during basic training included physical ones. When he entered the army Dad was healthy, but he clearly was not an athlete or an outstanding physical specimen. He was a slight man (probably about five feet, seven inches tall and little more than 125 pounds) and had poor eyesight (but not poor enough to keep him out of the army at that stage of the war). His major activities during his adolescence had been relatively sedentary—school, working for the newspaper, watching sporting events, listening to the radio, occasionally fishing and hunting. So the hard physical work of basic training and the long and grueling hours were definitely a shock to his system. On February 8, he writes of how the physical regimen is coloring his views of army life, though he chooses to censor himself for the benefit of his mother and sister: "Currently, my opinion of the army— ______ ______ ______ ______ ______. In fact, I hate the ______ ______ army. After working hard all day long, we went on a forced 3-hour march tonight with steel helmet, rifle, battle pack, and all the trimmings. This is the first time off we have had since 6:15 this morning."

Things hadn't improved much by the next day, for on February 9 he writes of "another long hard day today. Army motto is evidently 'Work 16 hours a day, police area 4 hours a day, make beds 4 hours a day, and sleep 8 hours a day.' Hey, that's 32 hours to a day." But over the next several weeks, he started looking around at how others were doing, and he put the physical work into perspective. Some of what he learned confirmed previous doubts about himself, but he also began to see his physical capability in a new light. For example, on February 15 he writes, "We did a lot of double-timing (running) today, with rifles & packs (I'm starting to feel as though that pack were part of me.) I found out I was pretty soft—can't take much of it. Compared to some of the 30 or 35 year olds, though, I'm hard as nails. This training is really killing them by degrees."

A little more than a week later, on February 23, he uses his observations of others as motivation, noting that "about 1/3 of the company is limping around, half sick, falling out when we start double-timing. *Me*—I'm going to keep the pace up until I drop unconscious." By the end of the next month, on March 30, he is marveling at his success in physical activities, and notes how they make him less and less of a civilian: "Say, Pop, I won't be able to go walking with you when I get home. These speed marches are ruining my walk. Even when I go for a pleasure jaunt I practically run away with myself. You know how the calves of my legs used to be? Rather flabby & large? Well they are now hard as rocks & a lot smaller. Speed marches!"

All this increased exercise was accompanied by an increased appetite. Dad often wrote about food in his letters—the menu for the day, extra eating at the service club and dayroom—and he made requests for food from home to add to the stash in his footlocker. Early on in his training, on February 13, he notes his mixed approval of army chow: "Now, the food situation—plenty of meat, well-cooked—good salads—just fair vegetables—desserts not so good—coffee to drink. I'm learning to eat big breakfasts—usually bacon & eggs, cereal, toast, coffee, & an orange." He describes himself as eating "like a mad hungry dog—(which I am)—every mealtime." And the voracious eating often extended beyond mealtime. On February 17 he reports, "Was down at PX about an hour ago, just after classes. I consumed—(1-) 1 bottle Pepsi-Cola—(2-) 1 pint chocolate milk—(3-) one small 5¢ cake—& (4-) one package crackers & peanut butter. That after a good supper. Don't worry about me getting sick, though. I've been eating like a couple horses & it hasn't affected me a bit—except to make me feel good. Also rapidly devouring your wonderful candy, Mom."

By the end of April, after three months of huge eating and intense exercise and when the end of basic training was in sight, Dad's physical transformation seemed to be complete. After a leave he writes home, "While I was in Ocala I weighed myself on 3 scales. Each one agreed—*148 pounds.* Allowing 5 pounds for clothes, that means I have gained 18 pounds since coming into the army. I wonder if I'm really me."

Physical conditioning was one major element of World War II infantry training; weapons instruction was the other. Though soldiers in the very early stages of the war trained on such weapons as the World War I-era Springfield rifle, by 1943 the standard armaments for the rifle companies of infantry units included the .30 caliber M1 Garand rifle, the .30 caliber U.S. carbine, the Thompson submachine gun, the Browning machine gun, and heavy weapons such as mortar and bazookas.[9] My father was given limited training on several of these weapons. He tells of firing a bazooka (a "marvelous instrument of tank destruction"), firing off antitank grenades from his rifle ("You really have to hold it tight or you'll be knocked clear off your feet by the terrific recoil. It really jars a fellow up"), and of training with hand grenades and in gas drills. However, his most extensive weapons training, like most infantrymen's, was on the M1, the rifle soldiers learned to fire from an assortment of firing positions in various situations and from various distances and learned to clean in whatever way possible (pipe cleaners were practically required; lighter fluid was a cleaning "cheat" that was tolerated if not encouraged). Though my father found out early on that he would be receiving specialized training as a radio operator, this did not excuse him from weapons training. The recruits who did not pass specialized code training (thirteen "words" per minute at the end of the thirteenth week) would be transferred back to a rifle company, and because soldiers in all parts of an infantry unit, including the headquarters unit, anticipated involvement in fighting, weapons training was essential.[10]

My father started this part of his training with a bit of trepidation. He felt reasonably confident about cleaning his rifle (on February 12 he wrote, "At rifle inspection, my pretty little M1 was used as an example of how to properly clean the bore. However, the Lt. found a few specks of sand in my rear sight") but less confident about firing it. Though he had experience hunting with his father, he was clearly worried about his ability to shoot well enough for the army. On February 16 he says, "Started rifle marksmanship today. I'm afraid of this subject—the company in the last cycle qualified 100%, & Capt. Williams expects us to do the same. You know me. I boloed U. of I. firing."[11]

Less than a week later, the rifle training had begun in earnest. Dad found it rough going at first, but he quickly got into the swing of it, although he may not have fully appreciated the seriousness of the undertaking. On February 21 he wrote home, "I about killed myself working on firing positions—especially sitting. Those positions really twist you all over the place & are very painful. This afternoon we started individual training—cover, concealment, crawling, etc. Practically all afternoon I crawled through heavy brush, palmettos, & sand—inching along at times, double timing, slamming down to the ground—all with packs & rifles. It was sort of fun, though—something like 'cowboys & Indians.'"

And early in March, Dad surprised himself by qualifying as a sharpshooter, first on his M1 ("I shot 4 bulls & 4 4's—& am I proud") and then on the carbine ("a beautiful little weapon—very light, easy to fire"). His pride in his own performance was matched by his pride in his platoon and company ("Our company shot the highest of any company *ever* in the 69th regiment") and his happiness over the perks that came with such success. On March 5 he writes, "To start with, I'll tell you about last week. I, as stated in yesterday's letter, am a *sharpshooter*—with 169 out of a possible 210. Just 11 points short of expert, the highest rating. Our platoon was the best in the company, so we don't have to stand reveille next week. That means instead of having to report outside as soon as we get dressed, we can wait till first formation at 7:30. Our company was the best in the regiment, also."

Thus, in the areas most critical to becoming an effective U.S. Army infantryman—physical conditioning and weapons training—my father surprised himself with his achievements in the first seven weeks of basic training. However, in his initial classification interview on arriving at Camp Blanding, he had been assigned to radio school, so his specialized training in radio would be critical to his success at the base. In an early letter responding to a sort of questionnaire from his parents, Dad described the possible implications of the radio training:

> *Q—Do you know where you would be sent if & when you pass the radio exam there?*
>
> *A—There are several possibilities:*
>
> 1. *A small percentage—about 15—will go to Ft. Benning for advance training. I don't expect to be good enough to go with these.*
> 2. *A large percentage will be attached to headquarters detachments & shipped overseas immediately as radiomen. There is a strong possibility I may go over but not see action.*
> 3. *Some are stationed at various camps in this country. I hope I'm one of this group.*

These responses show that Dad was trying to reassure his parents about his possible assignments and to discourage any hopes they might have that he would distinguish himself in radio school. His attempt to lower expectations was probably self-protective, to make himself (and his parents) feel better about whatever level of performance he achieved. It was also prudent, as a number of men in his unit already had some, or even extensive, background in radio transmission, making it harder to break into the top 15 percent that would go on for further training at Ft. Benning. As soon as training started on

March 7, however, Dad began to feel both an affinity toward code and a talent for it. On the first day of training he writes,

> *We had about 6 hours code. I think I'm going to like it. We already know about 15 characters. Had a test at 5 words per minute (words = code groups of 5 characters. Not regular words) & got all o.k. in the 2 minutes. Some of the guys (most of them, in fact) missed up to 75% of the characters.*
>
> *Already I'm "dit-happy." We learn the code as "dit"—dot & "dah" = dash. Besides singing code "dit-dit-dit-dah" we also whistle it to each other. Intriguing work!*

A week later, on March 15, he reports his first major word-per-minute success in code: "I am honored to report—and happy—that I have passed 5 W.p.m. today. I & about 9 others *without* previous experience have passed 5 & are working on 6 now. About 15 others *with* previous experience are working as high as 14 W.p.m. That leaves around 150 still on 5 W.p.m." He continued to progress in his code training, though there were some moments of frustration. On March 22 he notes that he almost passed 8 wpm but got so nervous at the end of the test that his hand was shaking. On March 27, however, he writes that "your worthy son made himself a little more worthy today by passing 8 W.p.m. & joining that select little group of 10 W.p.m. men." Two days later, he passed the 10 wpm test and later worked through the levels of 12 wpm (April 10), 14 wpm (April 11), 16 wpm (May 3), and 18 wpm before officially graduating from training. He ended his code training at Blanding as "the highest man without previous experience," and on April 20 he shows off his skills by sending a request home via code:

• • •	- - -	• • •		- •	•	•	- • •
S	*O*	*S*		*N*	*E*	*E*	*D*

- -	- - -	• - •	•
M	*O*	*R*	*E*

• - - •	•	- •	- • - •	• •	• - • •	• • •
P	*E*	*N*	*C*	*I*	*L*	*S*

Thus, as my father's period of basic training at Camp Blanding wound down, his assumption of the role of soldier was becoming complete, and, by his account, he had surprised himself with his success in many areas. He was at least keeping up with the training and had seen a physical transformation such that he wondered if the body he inhabited was really his. He had succeeded in his tests of basic soldiering, achieving "marksman" status on all weapons and contributing to the overall success of his platoon and company. In his specialized radio training in code, he was very successful, and he thought it likely that he would be able to move on to advanced training at Camp Benning, Georgia. However, it was critical that his successes in adapting to the role of soldier be accompanied by a separation from his old social world in civilian life.

When my father had first arrived at Camp Blanding, he had been horribly homesick and worried about making friends. In his initial assignment on arrival, his barracks was filled with older men ("between 31 and 38 and married—so I've been pretty darned lonely") and he had despaired of ever getting over the homesickness ("cried last night, dammit"). But within days a few recruits arrived to whom he felt a closer connection. On February 3 he had written, "Among the new men who came in, there is a redhead from St. Louis in the bunk next to mine. He was at Kansas U. with the ASTP before coming here—*and* he was a good friend there of Tommy Hamilton—a Champaign kid—and Jack Gordon." Soon, he started making friends with others who seemed more like him (Joe Dibrell—who "plays chess," Chuck Jones—a "good-humored student," Cal Melson and Gene Hill—"two swell fellows," and Tom Mallow—"One of the best. Likes to read, write. We get into some hot baseball arguments. A real pal"). Of course, there were many soldiers he did not like—sometimes the older men, and often those who were especially interested in drinking, gambling, and womanizing. But over the weeks, he found his place among the younger recruits, especially those with interest in education and those who were also in training for code. He even described—with great glee—a night during which he and his buddies short-sheeted the beds of other recruits and engaged in other time-honored barracks pranks.

As my father worked his way through basic, though, he did not fully relinquish his civilian identity. He wrote his folks that he continued to "think too much" and to miss his family and home town. He coped with this homesickness by taking out a subscription to the *News-Gazette* and avidly following sports results from Illinois high schools, the Big Ten, and the Chicago Cubs. His correspondence was directed not only to his mother and father, but to both his sisters and to neighbors and family friends. On April 12 he added a P.S. to his letter, saying, "Boys here have started calling me 'Chamber of Commerce Miller, the home-loving boy.' That's because I talk about home, you folks, & Urbana all the time." But there were also signs of letting go. He subscribed to *Yank* but sent the magazines back home so that his family would understand his life as a soldier. As he says on April 1, "I can read it anytime. Copies all over the place." When his parents divulged plans to move into a house in Urbana, he wrote (on March 19), "From your wonderful architectural drawings, I can see that the new house will be fine, Mom. Which bedroom is 'mine'—or the 'guest room,' whichever you prefer to call it?"

At the end of his training at Camp Blanding as all were awaiting their orders for the next stage of training, my father went to Jacksonville on a short leave with some friends. His description of his trip reveals a young man independent enough to be off on his own after successfully completing his basic training, but still holding on to the sensibilities of his Midwestern boyhood. On June 4 he writes,

> *Now comes the good part—we were standing on the corner wondering what to do, when a good-looking Marine & a blonde little sailor asked us to go to a wiener roast with them at a place about 5 miles outside town. Said a couple sailors stood them up. They looked like good kids so we went along.*
>
> *We went to a very nice country home, & met 7 girls, 2 more sailors, & another Marine. We sure had a lot of fun. It was a mixed party—no one with anyone in particular. Had wieners, marshmallows, & lemonade. Also some delicious home-made ice cream. The kind you make in a freezer.*
>
> *Left there about 11 & went back to town to catch a bus. The line for the bus was pretty long, so we went to a midnight show. Finally got back to camp at 4:30 this morning.*
>
> *Ain't I a playboy, though? I feel it was a little justified, as 17 weeks' training was over & a celebration was in order.*

So at the beginning of June 1944, my father was awaiting word of where he would be sent in the next phase of army life. There had been many rumors about the effect of age on orders, the possibility of furloughs, and whether those shipping overseas would be heading to Europe or to the Pacific. Because of his strong performance in code, Dad felt certain that he would be sent to Ft. Benning, Georgia, for advanced training. Though he was disappointed that this might mean no opportunity to go home ("Lt. Levy told me yesterday it is highly unlikely that the Benning men will get furloughs") he told his family that they could work out a visit from Illinois to Georgia ("So you better start packing, for as soon as I get settled, you're coming down. That's an order"). The first set of orders for his cohort of soldiers arrived the first weekend in June, but my father was not concerned that he was not included in that set. On June 4 he wrote, "About 50 men in the company have received their orders. All are bound for Ft. Meade (a P.O.E.) [port of embarkation] & have from 17 to 23 days delay enroute. A very nice furlough. Steve is one of them. He leaves Tues. Kressley leaves Wed. and so does Pohlmann. No Benning orders are down yet—& some Meade orders aren't down. So I sit & wait."

The next day, though, June 5, he was not so sanguine: "Well, now I am going nuts. Everyone but about 15 men in the company have their orders. And I'm one of the 15. The Benning orders came down today. About 50 men, but *not me.* It is very puzzling. A lot of good men are going to Benning, & also several 14 & 16 W.p.m. operators. But me on 20, Gus Gavras on 20, Bob Maples on 20, & Mike Polakunich on 22 didn't get orders. . . . So I don't know where I'm going or when I'm going. Red, Jack, Joe D., & Kurt are all going to Benning. To further my disappointment, the Benning men are getting 10-day furloughs."

And by later that week (June 8) he was reduced to sending a brief and angry missive:

Dear Folks,
Short letter.
I'm mad, disgusted, etc.
No orders.
No mail.
Everyone but me & a few leaving.
K.P. tomorrow.
Grrrrr—foo—etc.
Bye
Love
Bud

He still didn't know his fate several days later, but began to understand why he hadn't been assigned to Benning with his friends and others who had performed well in radio and code at Camp Blanding. A month and a half before, on April 19, he had written home, "Well, I found out today I'm *not* physically fit for overseas duty—at least at the present time. . . . The sterling army doctors told me my eyes were too bad—which I knew—& that my tonsils were infected—which I didn't. Anyway, right now I don't go over." The situation had evidently been cleared up a few weeks later, though. On May 2, he writes:

Well, this morning I was sent to the hospital for a recheck on my overseas physical. The following conversation ensued between the doctor and I.

Dr.—"What's wrong with you."
Me—"I guess I'm here because of my tonsils."
Dr.—"How far are you in basic?"
Me—"12 weeks."
Dr.—"Hell, you've lived this long, I guess you can live 5 more weeks. Next."
Ain't that a farce, though?

Sadly, it was a farce that kept him out of advanced radio school with his closest buddies from basic training. On June 10 he writes, "I think I know why I was scratched from the Benning list. It was my tonsils. Evidently I was still in Class B at the time the list was up for approval, because I was sent to the hospital Fri. morning for a checkup. After waiting 2 ½ hours, the doc looked at my throat and wrote 'Class A' on my papers. Now I don't know where they'll ship me. Maybe straight to Meade or Ord and on across. I'll call as soon as I know where & when I'm going."

Apparently he did call shortly after this letter, having learned that he was being sent—at least temporarily—to Fort Meade in Maryland. From the dates on his letters, it is also apparent that he had enough time en route to go back to Illinois for a two-week visit with his family. In the next letter, dated June 30, he reports, "I arrived here at Meade at 10 o'clock, a pretty sick kid. I guess it was a combination of the train & bus ride, and homesickness. Mostly the latter, I suspect, because I don't know a soul here yet. . . . I feel like I did the first few days at Sheridan. On the verge of bawling all the time." He stayed at Camp Meade for only a week, and although he was still homesick, he enjoyed the "liberal pass policy," saw a bit of Washington, DC, and took in a few Washington Senators baseball games. But then he was back on the train again, heading for his next post. When he arrived at Camp Van Dorn, Mississippi, on July 10, he was not at all happy with the assignment: "Dear Folks, Well, I'm in the ______ ______ South again—and am I ever disgusted."

★ ★ ★

CAMP VAN DORN, located near Centreville, Mississippi, was established in 1942 as U.S. involvement in World War II ramped up, and the camp served as a training base for soldiers for only a few short years. Indeed, it was declared "surplus" in October 1945, before my father even returned from Europe.[12] Camp Van Dorn was built very quickly—contracts for it were established in February 1942, building began in June, and the first troops arrived in November. L. M. Caulfield, a local historian, notes that in these early days of the war, "this camp was not one of frills. It was often referred to as a 'Theatre of Operations Camp.' Come here, learn the business of killing and how to save your own life. Tar paper barracks was the norm, heated by coal heaters."[13] The first troops to train at Camp Van Dorn were soldiers from the 99th Infantry Division, who moved on from the camp in November 1943. Members of the 63rd Infantry Division began arriving in the late summer of 1943. L. M. Caulfield says that by this time, the camp had moved beyond its early days of tar-paper barracks. "Of course, the 63rd moved into an established camp—beautiful place . . . but I understand there [were] some disgruntled soldiers!"[14]

"Disgruntled" understates my father's initial negative reaction to Camp Van Dorn. On July 12 he writes, "I saw a Walter Winchell column posted on a bulletin board near here. This item was circled, 'People should spare a little sympathy for the boys at Camp Van Dorn, Miss.' Boy, is he right. This place is indeed a dry hole." Two days later, he notes that dissatisfaction with the camp is widespread: "The situation in this camp & company is getting pretty desperate. Another man in our 25-man barracks went AWOL last night. He left this note, 'Back in two weeks—Love & kisses, Stan.'" And on July 26, he adds a PS to his letter: "Very *dirty* joke I heard today—If you were to give the U.S. an enema, you would insert the tool at Camp Van Dorn, Miss."

My father's attitude toward Camp Van Dorn was just one aspect of his general misery at this stage of his training. His first five weeks in Mississippi were clearly the low point for his spirits during stateside training. He suffered from severe homesickness. On July 12, in one of three letters he wrote home that day, he complains, "This place sure makes me feel like hell. I'm so homesick I'm about to go crazy." The next day he writes, "Every time I turn around I curse this army & the war. Everyone in the barracks seems to enjoy himself a little, but I sure can't while I'm away from you folks." And the next day: "I'm still awfully lonely & homesick. . . . Gee, do I miss home. I sure wish the Russians would hurry up & take Berlin & we'd take Tokyo, so this blasted war would be over." Apparently, the family back in Urbana were very worried by this series of letters, since a few days later, on July 17, Dad writes, "I'm sure sorry if I've caused you folks a lot of worry with my letters. From now on I'll try to write more cheerful letters." But he obviously had trouble following through on this promise as he begins the very next paragraph with, "I've given up all hope of finding any friends, & have decided to devote my energy to reading and writing."

There were probably a number of reasons for my father's increased homesickness during this period. First, he was just returning from a visit back to

Urbana, so his longing for home life was particularly pronounced. Second, Camp Van Dorn clearly wasn't the pleasantest of environments, especially in the middle of the summer with Mississippi heat and humidity bearing down on him and chiggers biting at him, and it fell far short of Camp Blanding and its extensive facilities. Third, in Dad's early days at Camp Van Dorn, there just wasn't a lot to do. He had to wait on his gear, and he spent a lot of time working on details and sitting around. He was bored.

In fact, boredom must have been a common problem among men who spent much of their time waiting, who were doing work in which they were not intrinsically interested, and who were doing it again and again, in the repetitive practice that would enable them to perform tasks rapidly and by rote under battlefield conditions. Practice must sometimes have been mind-numbing. "If there was anything more goddamn bloody boring than the infantry," Ray Wax says in *"The Good War,"* "I don't know what it is. How many times can you break down a machine gun and reassemble it?"[15]

But the biggest factor figuring in my father's unhappiness and homesickness was his lack of friends and his feeling that the others at the camp were very different from him and the buddies he had had at Camp Blanding. On July 12 he writes, "All the men in the barracks have had at least 20 months in the army, & most of them have ratings. To them, I'm just so much mud, to be treated as such. In their eyes, the only thing I'm good for is to do details. I don't think I'll ever like the place or the men. If I had just *one* friend I might be alright, but I haven't. I suppose the only thing I'll ever do around here are the dirty jobs no one else likes to do."

And on July 16, he continues along the same lines: "At the end of basic at Blanding I was beginning to feel a bit like a man, but down here among these vets & noncoms I feel cowed, & seem to be just a child, not yet matured in mind—or body either, for that matter. The men's interests are so much different from my own. They want to be drunk all the time, forever be with women, married or otherwise, & have no interest at all in reading or education."

Luckily, though, my father's gloom didn't last forever. By the end of July, he was feeling somewhat better. He had developed friendships with several young men a lot like himself, so he had buddies to pal around with at the movies or on passes off base. He became especially close to Harold West, a "good-natured" kid from Wisconsin. Further, he began his field exercises, so he had less time to think. On July 19 he writes, "Boy, folks, I was sure glad to get to work in the field. It really took my mind off things, for a while at least." And the next day he adds, "Naturally, I'm still homesick, but it only pops out visibly when I'm idle—& believe me I'm not going to be idle very much." Finally, near the end of July, he found a way to regain some of the sense of competence he had felt at Camp Blanding. Because of the glut of radio operators at Camp Van Dorn, he was assigned to the message center rather than radio, but he was successful there and was even "borrowed" for extra stints in various offices and as a backup radio operator.

And he again surprised himself by excelling at the physical aspects of army life. On July 27 he could report with satisfaction, "I'm gaining quite a reputation around here for strength and endurance. I'm the only one who can stand up under the marches & still have the energy left for what is considered hard work around here." And on August 4, he makes a proud announcement: "Now I'll give out with the good news. As you have probably guessed because of the return address, I am now a PFC.—Private First Class. That means I get $4 more per month and am entitled to wear 1 stripe. It was certainly a pleasant shock to me when Sgt. Atwood informed me of my promotion yesterday. . . . Forrest & Silberman were the only others to get their Pfc. Stripes. From now on, just address your mail to PFC. Joe T. Miller. I feel pretty good about the promotion."

During the remaining three months of my father's stay at Camp Van Dorn, he was marking time, but it was a busy period nevertheless. While his weeks in basic training at Camp Blanding had been full of learning experiences and physical development, activities at Camp Van Dorn were much more about consolidating soldiering skills in day-long or extended exercises. He described the discomfort and tedium of these days, as well as his roles in the message center, as code clerk, and as radio operator. Although it was clear that he would find a home in some capacity within the headquarters company of the regiment, precisely what capacity was unclear, since various higher-ups had conflicting ideas about what his position should be—an assortment of officers and noncoms requested him for their sections.

Dad also took part in the hubbub that engulfed the camp when reviews with Army brass were scheduled. On August 17 he writes, "Quite a day today—preparing all day for an inspection of the 63rd Division by Gen. Lear, commander of the Army Ground Forces, next week. Had close order drill, military courtesy all morning. Cleaned equipment & had a practice parade this afternoon. This Gen. Lear is a 'parade ground' general, from all reports. Doesn't care how good you are at your job, just so long as you appear to be wonderful drillers, dressers, etc. Therefore, the practice."

While off duty, Dad spent many evenings watching movies. In his letters he comments by name on twenty-five different films he saw at Camp Van Dorn and mentions outings to other, unnamed ones as well. Other evenings he spent tracking rumors about the future movement of his unit. The unit history of my father's 254th Regiment notes that during this period at Camp Van Dorn, "Dame Rumor became the new Commanding Officer as each barracks had its quota of those who either 'got it straight from a guy who practically runs division personnel' or 'was just down at S-1 when this phone call comes in, see.'"[16] Apparently my father was an active part of this grapevine, for in various letters he writes about "confirmed" reports that the 63rd Infantry Division will be part of the Army of Occupation, that they will be shipped to the Pacific, and that only older soldiers will be shipped overseas. The rumors ran rampant throughout the camp, as he reports on September 10:

> *Yesterday morning at our regular weekly orientation, Capt. Horlock, Intelligence officer, asked for rumors. Among those given, humorous and otherwise:*
>
> 1. *We're going to England to be Army of Occupation in Europe.*
> 2. *We're going to combat in the Pacific.*
> 3. *The division has ordered 5,000 surfboards & Hawaiian guitars, and we're going to Hawaii.*
> 4. *The division has 3,000 pair of snowshoes for use in Siberia.*
> 5. *The regiment just got in 200 pounds of maps of Denmark, and we're going there.*
> 6. *We're going to invade the Antarctic and drive out the penguins.*
>
> *So you see, no one really knows anything. As Capt. Horlock said, "All I know is that we are going somewhere by the middle of October."*

As it turned out, everyone (including Capt. Horlock) was wrong.

Finally, in the last months of training, Dad was determined to find a way to see his family again before the next phase of army life. He initially explored ways to get back to Illinois on a three-day pass, but decided that such a plan would be unworkable. He then devised a detailed scheme for getting his family to visit him. On August 13 he writes,

> *Here's my plan for you coming down—or just you, Dad, if you feel Mom & Judy couldn't make the trip. Buy a round trip ticket to Macomb, Miss. Come down on a train that gets here Sat. afternoon or evening on Sept. 2. Let me know the time & I'll try to meet you at the station. I'll get a room for us Sat. nite. Then I'll get a room for you at the guest house on the post for Sun. & Mon. nites. Tues., Wed., & Thurs. I'll get a 3-day pass—we'll go to New Orleans maybe. Friday nite you can get a room in Centreville. Sat. we might go to*

> *Natchez, Miss., or maybe Vicksburg. Then Sun. night you can get a train out of Macomb at 10:15 which will get to Champaign the next afternoon.*

Apparently my grandfather decided that this trip was not feasible, as the strategy soon shifted to using a series of passes to travel back to Illinois. But these plans too were cancelled when visiting dignitaries got in the way and a twenty-eight-day exercise was planned for almost the full month of October. But Dad's hopes had been raised again when he wrote on September 30, "I typed up the list of names of men still eligible for furlough yesterday. My name is the last one on the list. I confirmed the report that I would get my leave the last of October by asking the First Sgt. I probably won't be home for my birthday, but I am certainly not going to turn down any furlough, no matter when it is offered me."

On October 2, he still anticipated a furlough at the end of the month, as he closes his letter with "see you in 3 or 4 weeks." But apparently things started moving fast, and plans changed yet again. The unit history recalls that at this time "the great exodus for the train station at McComb began as mass furloughs were granted. After our hectic ten days at home, wives, mothers, and sweethearts were left in tears at the station as we departed with the 'this is it' attitude."[17] My father apparently received one of these furloughs, as his next letter is dated October 16, and it is clear that he is returning from a trip back to Illinois: "I got here o.k. Arrived in camp about 8:30 tonight. . . . Naturally, I'm pretty blue right now—probably will be for a week or so. However, I'm not near so sick as I was when I left before." And from then on, business at Camp Van Dorn took on a new urgency. This is part of Colonel James Hatcher's account of the 63rd Infantry's preparatory activities:

> *The last few days at the home station were particularly busy. After the packing and crating came preparation of orders for the movement to the entraining area and orders for the entraining of men and equipment. Such orders must be prepared with an exactness that permits train after train to move into and out of the entraining area without delay and with a minimum time interval between trains. Then there was the organization of command, kitchen and messing facilities aboard trains, and the final and minute inspections of all required activities including the last showdown inspections to insure that each man was equipped to the last shoelace.*[18]

My father's descriptions of these days suggest that he was actively involved in many of the preparations:

- *October 21: "Well, things are really humming down here. . . . It looks like we are getting ready to go places—where no one knows."*
- *October 25: "Boy, I have really been busy, as has everyone else in this company. There is an awful lot of work connected with this moving business."*
- *October 27: "That orderly room where I'm working now is a veritable madhouse. And we're drawing our new clothes & have orders to send our civvies stuff home."*
- *October 29: "I've certainly brushed up on my shorthand & typing in the past week working in the orderly room. There has been a terrific amount of paperwork to do, & I've done most of it."*
- *October 30: "Latest reports set this Sunday as the day we pull up stakes and take off."*
- *November 1: "This afternoon the communications platoon was evacuated from its barracks in order to get room to store all our post equipment. They split us up, 1/3 to each other platoon. I'm now with the message center group in the A & P barracks. It is was quite a little work moving."*
- *November 3: "We've been turning in stuff, drawing stuff—inspection, inspection, inspection—& between times I've been typing in the orderly room. Quite a busy boy I've been."*

In the midst of all this busyness, my father continued to update his family on news of rumored destinations, in spite of his comment on October 27 that "we got censorship instructions today—they told us not to say anything to anyone—but of course you know everything anyway." The initial destination was determined to be the New York point of embarkation; then it was on to Europe. (October 25: "Soon I'll be able to write you from Piccadilly & listen to the chimes of historic Big Ben.") He also continues to reassure his parents that his assignment should not involve any danger, as he anticipates being part of the Army of Occupation and not in battle. He goes so far as to write **DON'T WORRY!!!** in script that takes up half the page.

On November 4 he writes, "I'm down to mere basic clothing now. And sleeping on a mattress without a bed under it. All set." Two days later, on November 6, he was part of the advance party of the 63rd Infantry Division (253rd, 254th, and 255th Regiments) that was entrained out of Camp Van Dorn under the command of Brigadier General Frederick M. Harris, en route to Camp Shanks, New York. Bud's basic training was complete. He was on his way to war.

Joe's mother, Irene Snyder, as a young woman.

The Miller family, circa 1933. Irene, Dorothy, and Oscar are in the back row. Judy and Joe are in front.

Joe and Judy on a well-loved bike, circa 1936.

Oscar Francis Miller, circa 1938.

Oscar Miller (left) with employee Tom at the print shop, circa 1940.

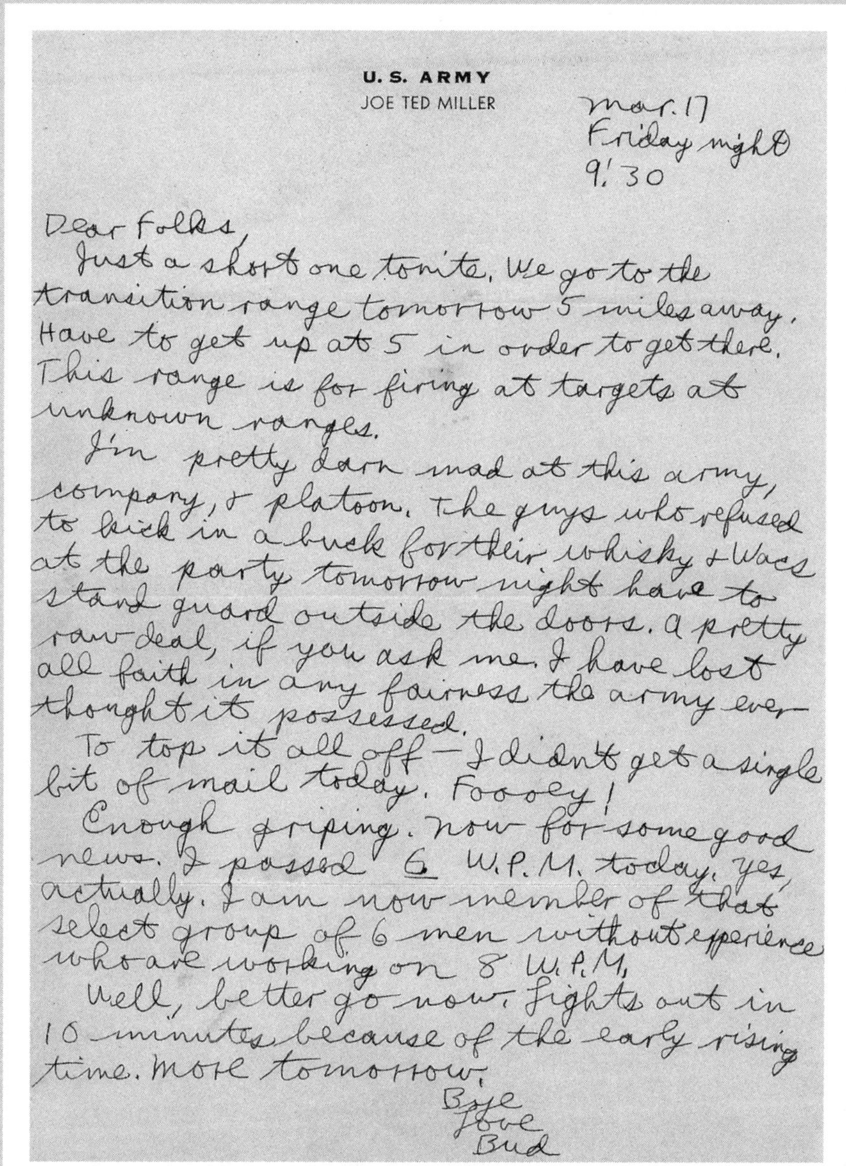

U.S. ARMY
JOE TED MILLER

Mar. 17
Friday night
9:30

Dear Folks,

Just a short one tonite. We go to the transition range tomorrow 5 miles away. Have to get up at 5 in order to get there. This range is for firing at targets at unknown ranges.

I'm pretty darn mad at this army, company, & platoon. The guys who refused to kick in a buck for their whisky & Wacs at the party tomorrow night have to stand guard outside the doors. A pretty raw deal, if you ask me. I have lost all faith in any fairness the army ever thought it possessed.

To top it all off — I didn't get a single bit of mail today. Foooey!

Enough griping. Now for some good news. I passed 6 W.P.M. today. Yes, actually. I am now member of that select group of 6 men without experience who are working on 8 W.P.M.

Well, better go now. Lights out in 10 minutes because of the early rising time. More tomorrow.

Bye
Love
Bud

A typical handwritten letter, sent from Camp Blanding, Florida, on March 17, 1944.

6 Nov 1944 - Entrained Camp Van Dorn Mississippi
9 No v1944 - Detrained Camp Shanks, New York
24 Nov 1944 - Entrained Camp Shanks, New York
24 Nov 1944 - Detrained and Embarked - Brooklyn Navy Yard
25 Nov 1944 - Sailed out of New Yo rk
8 Dec 1944 - Arrived Marseilles, France
9 Dec 1944 - Disembarked and Entrucked for C. P. 2 (Staging Area)
16 Dec 1944 - Entrained for Camp Oberhoffen (Bischweiller, France)
20 Dec 1944 - Arrived Camp Oberhoffen (Bischweiller, France)
30 Dec 1944 - Entrucked for Dieffenbach France
1 Jan 1945 - Arrived Hachimette France
8 Jan 1945 - Arrived Hunawihr France
16 Jan 1945 - Arrived Zellenberg France
23 Jan 1945 - Arrived Ribeauville Station France
25 Jan 1945 - Arrived Illhaeusern-Colmar Forest (Attacked Jebsheim France)
28 Jan 1945 - Arrived Jebsheim France
2 Feb 1945 Arrived Artzenheim France (0730)
2 Feb 1945 - Arrived Baltzenheim France (0730)
4 Feb 1945 - Arrived Artzenheim France
8 Feb 1945 - Arrived Jebsheim France
9 Feb 1945 - Arrived Enchenberg France
15 Feb 1945 - Companies arrived at Petit Rederching France
18 Feb 1945 - Arrived St. Michel France
19 Feb 1945 - Arrived Saargemines France
21 Feb 1945 - Arrived Neunkirchen France
7 Mar 1945 - Arrived AUERSMACHER "GERMANY"
15 Mar 1945 - Arrived Bliesransbach Germany
16 Mar 1945 - Arrived Ensheim Germany (Attacked Siegfried Line)
20 Mar 1945 - Arrived Ober-Wurzbach Germany
21 Mar 1945 - Arrived Neunkirchen Germany (Met 3d Army Troops)
22 Mar 1945 - Arrived Kirkel Germany
25 Mar 1945 - Arrived Langmeil Germany
28 Mar 1945 - Arrived in W[illegible] (2 Miles [illegible] Germany)
29 Mar 1945 - Arrived Mannheim Germany
5 Apr 1945 - Arrived Sindolsheim Germany (Attacked area to the South)
6 Apr 1945 - Arrived Merchingen Germany
8 Apr 1945 - Arrived Krautheim Germany (1300)
8 Apr 1945 - Arrived Marlach Germany (1930)
9 Apr 1945 - Arrived Dorrenzimmern Germany (Attacked area to the south)
10 Apr 1945 - Arrived Belsenberg Germany
12 Apr 1945 - Arrived Künselsau Germany
15 Apr 1945 - Arrived Mausdorf Germany
16 Apr 1945 - Arrived Kupferzell Germany (1130)
16 Apr 1945 - Arrived Kupfer Germany
17 Apr 1945 - Arrived Gottwollshausen Germany (1130)(Cont'd atk. to south)
17 Apr 1945 - Arrived Schwabish Hall Germany (1800)
19 Apr 1945 - Arrived Hassenfelden Germany (1100)(Con't atk. to south)
20 Apr 1945 - Arrived Steinbachle Germany (1230)
20 Apr 1945 - Arrived Unter-Aspach Germany (2000)
21 Apr 1945 - Arrived Hausen Germany
23 Apr 1945 - Arrived Unter-Groningen Germany (0230)
23 Apr 1945 - Arrived Unter-Böbingen Germany (1800)
25 Apr 1945 - Arrived Gerstetten Germany (0030)
25 Apr 1945- Arrived Reidheim Germany (1830) Crossed DANUBE River to Leipheim Germany (Reld from DRIVE)
28 Apr 1945 - Arrived Hoferstadt Germany (0100)
28 Apr 1945 - Arrived Ochsenfurt Germany (1400)
16 May 1945 - Arrived Kirchberg, Germany
21 May 1945 - Arrived (1) One Km. NE of Rudolfsberg, Germany(Bivouac Area)
26 May 1945 - Arrived Altenmunster, Germany

A typewritten list (found on onionskin paper with a carbon copy) of the movements of the 254th Regiment.

GI Joe—serving in the ETO in 1945.

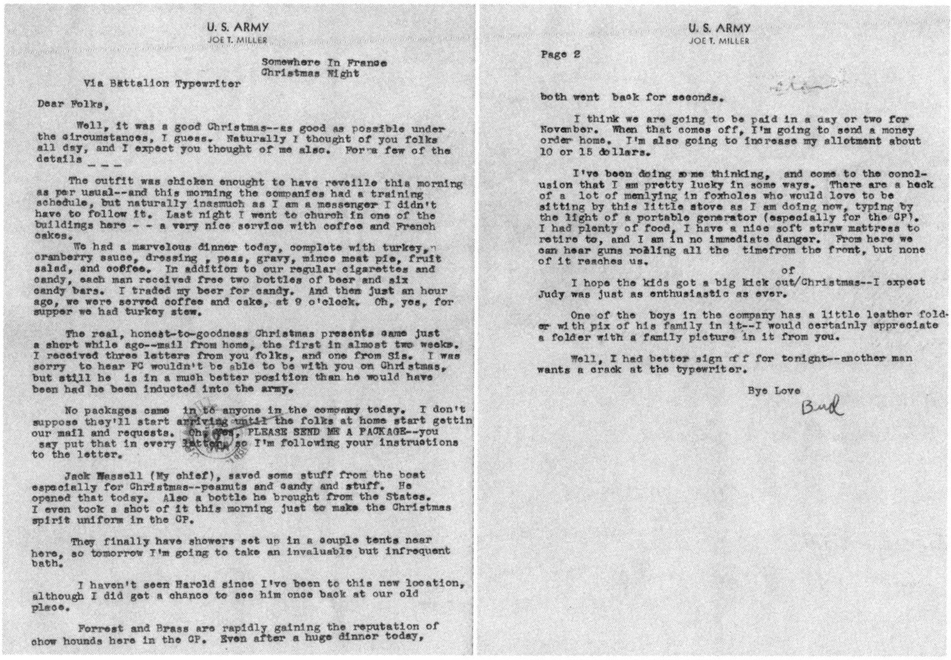

U. S. ARMY
JOE T. MILLER

Somewhere In France
Christmas Night

Via Battalion Typewriter

Dear Folks,

Well, it was a good Christmas--as good as possible under the circumstances, I guess. Naturally I thought of you folks all day, and I expect you thought of me also. For a few of the details _ _ _

The outfit was chicken enought to have reveille this morning as per usual--and this morning the companies had a training schedule, but naturally inasmuch as I am a messenger I didn't have to follow it. Last night I went to church in one of the buildings here - - a very nice service with coffee and French cakes.

We had a marvelous dinner today, complete with turkey, cranberry sauce, dressing , peas, gravy, mince meat pie, fruit salad, and coffee. In addition to our regular cigarettes and candy, each man received free two bottles of beer and six candy bars. I traded my beer for candy. And then just an hour ago, we were served coffee and cake, at 9 o'clock. Oh, yes, for supper we had turkey stew.

The real, honest-to-goodness Christmas presents came just a short while ago--mail from home, the first in almost two weeks. I received three letters from you folks, and one from Sis. I was sorry to hear PC wouldn't be able to be with you on Christmas, but still he is in a much better position than he would have been had he been inducted into the army.

No packages came in to anyone in the company today. I don't suppose they'll start arriving until the folks at home start gettin our mail and requests. Oh yes, PLEASE SEND ME A PACKAGE--you say put that in every letter, so I'm following your instructions to the letter.

Jack Massell (My chief), saved some stuff from the boat especially for Christmas--peanuts and candy and stuff. He opened that today. Also a bottle he brought from the States. I even took a shot of it this morning just to make the Christmas spirit uniform in the CP.

They finally have showers set up in a couple tents near here, so tomorrow I'm going to take an invaluable but infrequent bath.

I haven't seen Harold since I've been to this new location, although I did get a chance to see him once back at our old place.

Forrest and Brass are rapidly gaining the reputation of chow hounds here in the CP. Even after a huge dinner today,

U. S. ARMY
JOE T. MILLER

Page 2

both went back for seconds.

I think we are going to be paid in a day or two for November. When that comes off, I'm going to send a money order home. I'm also going to increase my allotment about 10 or 15 dollars.

I've been doing some thinking, and come to the conclusion that I am pretty lucky in some ways. There are a heck of a lot of menlying in foxholes who would love to be sitting by this little stove as I am doing now, typing by the light of a portable generator (especially for the CP). I had plenty of food, I have a nice soft straw mattress to retire to, and I am in no immediate danger. From here we can hear guns rolling all the timefrom the front, but none of it reaches us.

I hope the kids got a big kick out/of Christmas--I expect Judy was just as enthusiastic as ever.

One of the boys in the company has a little leather folder with pix of his family in it--I would certainly appreciate a folder with a family picture in it from you.

Well, I had better sign off for tonight--another man wants a crack at the typewriter.

Bye Love

Bud

A typewritten letter sent Christmas night, 1944, from Camp Oberhoffen, France.

Tourists in Paris, 1945. On the back Joe writes, "The arrows denote Nielsen and myself. This is a sightseeing group in front of the Arc de Triomphe. That's my camera I have in my hand."

Joe ready for his University of Illinois graduation, 1949.

Joe at the University of Texas campus (probably for a football game), 1950.

Bachelor party with the copydesk gang at the Detroit Free Press, *March 1953.*

Joe with his mother, summer of 1954.

Joe and Margaret Miller with their girls, 1964. Joe in the back, with Ann, Margaret, Mary, and Barb in the middle and Kathy in front.

The news desk gang at the Detroit Free Press, *late 1970s. Chris Kartesz, John (last name unknown), Jo Charles, Albert "Tick" Klock, Joe Miller, Bob McKelvey, and Chris Carey.*

CHAPTER TWO

Bud Goes to War

AS I WENT THROUGH the box of my father's letters, I came across two tissue-thin pieces of onionskin paper—a typed document and its carbon copy. The document is a list of dates and locations beginning with "6 Nov 1944—Entrained Camp Van Dorn Mississippi" and ending with "26 May 1945—Arrived Altenmunster, Germany." All told, this list of dates and locations contains fifty-eight entries. After those marking arrival at and departure from Camp Shanks, New York, and one that reads "Sailed out of New York," the entries note "entrainment," "entruckment," and arrivals at towns and villages in France and Germany. Sometimes hours are noted (in military time), especially if there was movement within a single day. Sometimes additional comments ("Attacked Siegfried line," "Met 3d Army Troops," "Crossed Rhine River") supplement the list, which includes locations such as Ribeauville Station in France and Neunkirchen, Dorrenzimmern and Schwabish Hall in Germany. When I found these onionskin documents, I assumed that my father had kept a personal record of all of his locations. Later, resource materials from the 63rd Infantry Division Association revealed that the official record of the 254th Regiment movements in the European theater of operations (ETO) was this exact list—word for word. This confluence of the official record and my father's effects is just one example of the layers of accounts I have met with in my effort to understand my father's experiences in Europe from December 8, 1944, until late March 1946.

In that effort, I have relied on multiple narratives about the 254th Battalion of the 63rd Infantry Division. Some of these are first-person accounts. The most relevant of them, of course, is the record provided by my father in his letters, but this account was constrained by official censorship rules and by what I suspect was Dad's desire to shield his family from the more grueling and sometimes dangerous aspects of his wartime life. Dad also had a small datebook that included very short daily entries from January 1, 1945, until May 5, 1945 (three days before V-E Day). I assume that many or most of the comments in it were made retrospectively, as in a letter dated February 16, 1945, Dad asked his father to send him a "little book to keep addresses and a travel log in"; and the entries are very abbreviated and usually in the past tense (for instance, for Wednesday, February 7: "Kane still First Sgt.—Chow still bad—Artzenheim a rather dirty little town. I did get a much needed shower there"). Other first-person accounts come from remembrances of soldiers of the 63rd Division published in the *Blood and Fire* newsletter and from an interview I conducted with one of my father's wartime buddies, Carl Brass, on June 13, 2009.[1]

In addition to these first-person archives, I have relied on historical accounts of the activities of the 254th Regiment and the 63rd Infantry Division. Closest to my father's own experiences are those recorded in the booklet *The Trail of the 254 thru Blood and Fire,* written in 1945 by Harris Peel, another member of the 254th and a friend of Dad's.[2] This booklet, one of many regimental histories written at the close of World War II, can be seen as both a record of unit activities and, at times, a public relations device extolling the bravery and virtues of unit soldiers. From a higher level in the army hierarchy is the account written by James E. Hatcher in 1972.[3] Colonel Hatcher was the executive officer of the 254th Regiment and, after March 21, 1945, commanding officer of the 255th Regiment. As the prologue to his book points out, "because of his duty assignments Colonel Hatcher was in a position to observe and record activities of important events within the division."[4] Additional information about the 63rd Infantry came to light at the Camp Blanding Museum and in records of troop movements, battle activities, and awards, which I obtained through the 63rd Infantry Division Association. Finally, from military histories such as Stephen Ambrose's *Citizen Soldiers,* Clarke and Smith's *Riviera to the Rhine,* and others, I acquired a broad view of specific battles my father was involved in (the Battle of Jebsheim in the Colmar Pocket and the breaching of the Siegfried line) and of military strategies and conditions on the ground in Europe.[5] Using all these accounts, ranging from the personal to the academic, it was possible to weave together the story of my father's experiences in the European theater.

Getting to the ETO

The other soldiers of the 63rd Infantry Division who entrained from Camp Van Dorn on November 6 were probably as happy to leave as my father was. Carl Brass, who spent many months at the camp, told me that the tar-paper barracks were "so cold that water underneath your bed would actually freeze on the floor."[6] The preparation for activation had been fierce, and Col. James Hatcher observed that "once on the train and under way, the first moment of complete relaxation in a period of several days was possible. Nothing more could be done by way of preparation."[7] As they were boarding the trains, most of the soldiers learned for the first time that they were heading for Camp Shanks, New York (noted in the headings of my father's letters as "Somewhere in New York"), and thus they also knew with certainty that they would be part of the ETO. The train ride took three days, during which my father appreciated the scenery that fled past his window and described it to the family. Of Virginia he notes on November 9, 1944, that "the towns and hamlets are so picturesque. Clean white houses—very unlike the typical South I have seen. Nice country."

The 63rd was at Camp Shanks for about two weeks as the division worked to qualify for shipping over to Europe. Harris Peel describes the time as "one of seemingly endless inspections, life-boat drill, must movies, and last minute range firing."[8] However, he also adds that passes were plentiful and that for soldiers without family in the area, "there was an endless pilgrimage from one bar to another, from one night spot to the next, from show to show with occasional stops at the Pepsi Cola bar for refreshment prior to another attempt to call home from the Serviceman's Telephone Exchange."[9] My father groused that he was not as much part of this activity as he would like. On November 11 he writes, "I've been more than busy inasmuch as I worked at Battalion typing till 10, & finished typing company rosters tonight. I don't like the deal I'm getting—everyone taking off to shows while I work, but I guess I'll just have to stand it." However, on November 15 (the day after his nineteenth birthday) he finally procured a pass and became "quite a shot cookie" after taking in all the sights and sounds of New York:

> *I did darn near everything yesterday. Jack Payne & I started off in Rockefeller Center & Radio City in the afternoon. They are really wonderful places, full of "modern design," all the latest conveniences, & huge buildings. We went to the top of the RCA building (70 stories up) & looked out over the city. A very nice view. Next we walked down Park Avenue—the ritziest & most exclusive street in N.Y.*
>
> *I left Jack about 6 in the evening—he went to Stamford, Conn. to visit his aunt there. I went to Toffeneti's on Broadway (remember the same place we ate at in Chicago, Dad?) for an excellent dinner. Then I went to Loew's State Theatre & saw a vaudeville show—top-flight vaudeville, too.*
>
> *At 8 o'clock I met Harold, as previously arranged. His pass started later than mine. We hopped the subway out to his cousin's apartment on E. 26th*

> *Street, from where I called you. The call was a wonderful birthday present to me, even if it was a day late.*
>
> *After that, we went, via "L," to the Staten Island ferry. We took the hour ride on the ferry, past the Statue of Liberty, to Staten Island. Then back up town for a bite to eat. Then we dropped in to see the picture "Wilson" about 2 a.m. An excellent Technicolor production dealing with the life of Woodrow Wilson.*
>
> *And, at last back to camp.*

About a week later, the 63rd left Camp Shanks for the Brooklyn Navy Yard. Col. James Hatcher mused that he had "often . . . wondered how many millions of men have darkly remembered the short trip from Camp Shanks, New York to the ferry, across the bay to the ship's side, and that agonizing climb up the gang plank to the deck of the transport. The shoulder straps cut into aching muscles, but arms and hands filled with luggage permitted no opportunity to relieve the strain."[10] My father, somewhat less elegantly, tells his folks that, on boarding the ship, he "was really all fagged out from carrying a heavy pack, a rifle, and duffle bag." However, he was extremely happy to be greeted by the Red Cross ladies with coffee (he drank six cups), doughnuts (he ate ten), and candy bars (he stashed four in his duffle). His gratitude leads him to admonish his family: "Don't scorn the Red Cross anymore, folks. I ceased to believe the wild, biased tales of their moneygrabbing when we were preparing to board ship."

Dad was also fortunate in his quarters aboard the troopship. Harris Peel reports that "each man was shown his stateroom, which consisted of one canvas bunk in a room with two hundred other canvas bunks."[11] But Dad was assigned to a stateroom with just four men, "two in lowers, two in uppers. Washing facilities, & even closets are in the rooms." These nice digs were available because the 63rd was being transported on the Saturnia, a converted Italian luxury liner. It had obviously seen better days—Carl Brass told me that "you could scrape the grime off the walls." But Dad tells his folks that the "food is fair, considering the conditions under which it must be prepared and served." According to Carl Brass, however, the Italian crew saved the good food for themselves, and the troops "got boiled potatoes and cabbage and an occasional piece of boiled beef, and we had to stand at tables and eat it." There were also conflicting reports about rough seas on the voyage. Howard Russell DeMar recalls that "those were the longest days I can remember; I was so seasick most of the time that the Rock of Gibraltar and the shore line at Marseilles looked like heaven to me."[12] Carl Brass recalls the journey as "very, very smooth. It was like going on a lake almost."[13] My father describes something between these extremes, writing that "one or two days were rough, but on the whole it has been smooth sailing. I just wish you folks were along on such a trip in peacetime."

After eleven days at sea, traveling in a convoy of twelve ships under steady speeds and in blackout conditions, the Saturnia passed through the Straits of Gibraltar. "To our left," Peel writes, "we could see a few lights blinking on 'The Rock' itself and the shadow it made from the light of the full moon; to our right it seemed as if the entire coastline of Northern Africa was a blaze of lights as our ship scurried through the mined waters."[14] Two days later, on December 8, 1944, the convoy arrived at Marseilles. Most of the convoy moved into the inner harbor, but "more than fifty sunken ships left by the retreating Germans effectively blocked the harbor to the Saturnia with her deeper draft."[15] However, in the calmer seas of the next morning, the Saturnia was able to slide up to and dock at the makeshift wharves of Marseilles.

Preparing for Battle

> Only those who were there can know. More than once in interviewing veterans of the January fighting, when I asked them to describe the cold, men have involuntarily shivered.
>
> STEPHEN E. AMBROSE, *Citizen Soldiers*

The 63rd Infantry Division docked at Marseilles on December 8, 1944, and the first camp location for the units was Staging Area Number 2, Delta Base Section. Getting there required a long march through the hills of suburban Marseilles, then an eighteen-mile truck ride along icy mountain roads. All commentators on Delta Base Section clearly agree that it was an absolutely miserable place. James Hatcher exclaims, "What a bleak prospect!"[16] and Harris Peel says, "No matter how cynical had been our expectation of what to expect at Staging Area Number 2, all of us were disappointed."[17] The area was a bald and barren rocky hill, punctuated only by rudimentary kitchen shacks and latrines. On the troops' arrival, the temperature was frigid and the wind was blowing, and their first task was to pitch pup tents in the frozen clay. I asked Carl Brass if this was difficult. His sardonic response: "Not if you like to drive pegs into a cement sidewalk."[18] In his first letter home from Europe, on December 12, 1944, my father summed up his reaction in a wry understatement: "I have become the first member of the family to set foot on foreign soil—and, doggone it, I don't care much about it." His next letter, two days later, includes a practical reaction to the weather: "Please send me a pair of earmuffs."

The 63rd spent one week at the staging area. During the days, they gathered equipment and supplies from ships or from other units. At night they tried to find ways to stay warm despite the limited shelter of pup tents. Some of the men built small fires for both warmth and light, but these, Harris Peel points out, proved problematic: "The first defensive action in which the regiment engaged was caused by a lone German observation plane which flew over our camp about three days after our arrival. In a matter of seconds all of the hundreds of fires which dotted our hill were extinguished and men who had always somehow gotten out of digging foxholes while in the States began to frantically make a personal entrenchment.[19]

On December 16, the units boarded trains at Pas De Lanciers for what my father describes in his diary as "a cold, crowded, miserable, 3-day train ride." The cars they boarded were "Hommes 40 et 8 cheveaux," known to Americans as "40 and 8" cars. These boxcars had been designed around the turn of the twentieth century to hold forty men and eight horses. Harris Peel recalled that "all of us laughed and wondered how either 8 horses or 40 men could be put in these tiny, ridiculous looking vehicles. We were not laughing nearly so hard a few minutes later when we learned that we were going to take a four day trip in these cars. Twenty-five men in each made for slightly crowded conditions, but it increased the much needed warmth considerably, there being no method of heating the box car."[20]

The train moved north through the French countryside, passing the towns of Lyon, Dijon, and Epinal. Looking out of the open boxcar doors, the soldiers saw the extensive destruction of buildings, roads, and bridges wrought by the German army. And they met French men, women, and children who were eager to make trades with them. "Cigarettes," Dad observed, "are the most valuable items to the French. Everyone, from 10 years old up smokes—and begs for cigarettes. Cute little French kids run alongside all Yank trucks yelling, 'cigarette, Joe.' One pack buys a quart of wine—8 cigarettes half a loaf of bread." The railroad ended at Saarburg, and the troops entrucked from there on December 20 to Camp Oberhoffen.

Camp Oberhoffen, translated into English as "Always Hope," was an old Napoleonic cavalry post. It had recently been retaken by the 79th Division, and signs of battle (like abandoned German equipment and the grave of the former German commander) were apparent. But accommodations were much better than those at the Delta Base staging area. Dad describes the barracks as "barnlike structures" and notes that the men in the wire section were able to hook up a portable generator—much appreciated both for warmth and to power a phonograph for piping music to the men. At this point, the 63rd Division was a part of Task Force Harris, with the 253rd and 255th Regiments on the line, though apparently with limited action. My father's regiment, the 254th, was officially in reserve.

As 1944 came to a close, then, my father spent Christmas in the bitter cold of the Alsace Lorraine region of France, in the suitably—or perhaps ironically—named "Camp Always Hope." There is little doubt that the soldiers felt a wide mix of emotions that Christmas—homesickness, fear, nostalgia, anxiety. But the reports I have of that holiday suggest that good food (turkey dinners plus extra provisions), a bountiful mail call, and nostalgic music won the day. From the perspective of more than sixty-four years, Carl Brass recalled that Christmas: "I can remember it was like you really got the feeling of Christ, because we were in a stable and I can remember the special service on the speakers, and they got some record players and they started playing White Christmas. And I can remember the record, 'I Will Remember You Always.' I don't think there was a dry eye in the whole place."[21] My father, not a religious man, also ruminates on the blessings of the day in a letter written Christmas night: "I've been doing some thinking, and come to the conclusion that I am pretty lucky in some ways. There are a lot of men lying in foxholes who would love to be sitting by this little stove as I am doing now, typing by the light of a portable generator (especially for the CP [Communications Platoon]). I had plenty of food, I have a nice soft straw mattress to retire to, and I am in no immediate danger. From here we can hear guns rolling all the time from the front, but none of it reaches us."

Three days later, on December 28, orders came attaching the 254th to the 3rd Infantry Division—which, James Hatcher recounts,

> *was a lone American division attached to the First French Army which had been engaged in a rather fruitless attempt to drive the Germans east of the Rhine and seize the line of the Rhine River from Strasbourg south to Switzerland. The rugged and bristling Colmar Pocket was in that area. The word* pocket *was one of those military understatements which commanders and journalists are apt to use to bolster the morale of their own fighting men. Unfortunately, the so-called Colmar Pocket was no pocket at all. It was a large and healthy bridgehead still held by the Germans west of the Rhine on the front of the Sixth Army Group.*[22]

On this December 28th, as the orders came down for the 254th, my father was still in a holiday mood. He writes: "Right now I'm listening to nostalgic music very remindful of home . . . A high-powered radio and a phonograph with a flock of records was purchased by the battalion back in the states, so we've got it set up here, with loud speakers piping music to the companies of the battalion. They just finished playing 'Stardust.' Makes one wonder why all battles aren't fought like this. In a warm room with soft music and a hot lemonade (made with K ration lemonade) to sip."

Within days, my father would clearly learn the difference between his ideal battle and the real one being fought nearby in the Vosges mountains. On New Year's Day, 1945, after a two- day truck ride, his regiment arrived at Hachimette, France. They were about to become part of the battle for the Colmar Pocket.

Days in Battle for the 254th

> At the beginning of the New Year, the GIs once again went on the offensive. They had rough terrain, the Siegfried line, mighty rivers, and deep ravines to cross, all defended by German soldiers fighting for their homeland. Conditions were miserable; it was one of the worst winters ever in Northwestern Europe. It was fought, in large part, by citizen soldiers who had been college students or high school graduates in 1944 and became frontline infantry in 1945.
>
> STEPHEN E. AMBROSE, *Citizen Soldiers*

My father arrived in Europe six months and two days after D-Day. In that half of a year, Allied forces first established a bridgehead in Normandy, then moved during the spring and summer to push the Germans back and take control of key cities in France and Belgium, including Paris and Antwerp. But many efforts were frustrating in the fall of 1945. "It took hard, brutal attritional battles to advance to the German West Wall defenses amid autumn mud and rain. While the Allies achieved several local penetrations of the West Wall, nowhere were they able to punch through the full depth of the German fortifications and achieve operational success."[23] During November, Patton's Third Army, Devers' Sixth, and Patch's Seventh all made progress in reaching the Rhine, with the exception of an area east of the river, in the Alsace region of France, that was still held by German forces. At the center of this pocket of land was the city of Colmar. For the Allied forces, it was important to straighten out the front line along the Rhine by eliminating the Colmar Pocket. "Shorter lines would mean fewer troops at the front, thus allowing the commanders of the three army groups to move more units back to the rear for rest and recuperation and, ultimately, to concentrate them for a final thrust into the German interior."[24]

But the straightening of this line would have to wait, because on December 16 Germany staged the counteroffensive in the Ardennes region that has come to be known as the Battle of the Bulge. Hitler had been thinking about this large surprise strike as early as mid-September;[25] his ambitious goal was to split Allied forces in the area and capture the city of Antwerp, ninety-three miles away. He timed the beginning of the Ardennes counteroffensive to coincide with forecasters' prediction of an extended period of overcast weather that would ground Allied air forces. The meteorological opportunity presented itself in mid-December, 1944, and the Battle of the Bulge began. Because of relatively low Allied troop strength in the Ardennes region and the surprise of the attack, the Germans had some initial small victories in the campaign, but these successes were limited. Indeed, one of the most famous incidents in this early period of the Battle of the Bulge occurred when German troops had largely surrounded the American 101st Airborne at Bastogne. The Germans invited the acting commander of the unit, Anthony McAuliffe, to surrender, and McAuliffe's terse and oft-quoted response was "Nuts!" Russell Hart and Stephen Hart summarize the upshot: "After this rebuff the initiative slowly slipped out of the Germans' grasp thanks to fierce American resistance, rapid commitment of substantial Allied reserves, and severe German logistic shortages."[26] Hitler, however, was not ready to admit defeat in the Ardennes, so at the dawn of the new year, he initiated an additional operation to the south, in the Alsace region of France. Hart and Hart describe it:

> *To help with this last-gasp effort to snatch success from the jaws of defeat, the* Westheer *initiated a diversionary attack, Operation Northwind, in Alsace-Lorraine on New Year's Eve 1944. The Germans intended that a thrust north from the Colmar Pocket—the German-held salient that jutted west over the Rhine into France—would link up at Strasbourg with a six-division attack south from the Saar. Although Hitler hoped that the attack would divert enemy reinforcements away from the Ardennes, in reality Northwind incurred heavy loses, yet only secured modest success and sucked few forces away from "the Bulge."*[27]

This, then, was the situation when the 254th arrived in Hachimette, having first been attached, along with the French First Army, to the 3rd Infantry Division, which was part of General Alexander Patch's Seventh Army. In the week or so prior to this, the 63rd Infantry Division had been involved in some combat as part of Task Force Harris, but the fighting involved only the 253rd and 255th Regiments, with the 254th in reserve. The 253rd and 255th continued in the northern region of Alsace as the Germans launched Operation Northwind. But the 254th went farther south to fight in battles in the Colmar Pocket and Jebsheim, France—fighting for which the regiment would be awarded a Presidential Unit Citation and the French Croix de Guerre.

The Colmar Pocket and the Battle of Jebsheim

A twenty-first century tourism website, visit-alsace.com, observes that "Alsace is an improbably beautiful place, uncharacteristically neat and tidy, the stuff of which fairy tales are made: medieval towns and villages with higgledy-piggledy, half-timbered houses alight in summer with cascading geraniums and petunias, south facing slopes neatly contoured with row upon row of vines; richly decorated wrought iron signs; great wooden doors from beneath which waft insistent, irresistible smells of onion tart, freshly baked bread, new wine, old barrels."[28]

It is unlikely that the men of the 254th would have described Alsace so idyllically as they entered battle there in January of 1945. Around them were not houses alight in riots of summer flowers, but instead bleak—if still beautiful—wintry mountains. And, my father writes, "it was really cold"; in fact, it was bitterly, bitingly cold. Stephen Ambrose's answer to his own rhetorical "How cold was it?" is a graphic "So cold that if a man didn't do his business in a hurry he risked a frostbitten penis."[29] And James Hatcher, with the 254th, notes that precautions were taken to guard against the serious danger of frostbite in other extremities: "Attempts were made to get dry socks for every man forward to front line positions, while drying and warming tents were set up in the mountains behind front line positions where a few men at a time could gather about a fire and dry their clothing."[30] There were no wafting smells of onion tarts or freshly baked bread in the Vosges Mountains during those wintry days, though the soldiers were happy to find that provisions left behind by village inhabitants could be used to augment the C rations and K rations issued by the military.

During the first three weeks of January, the soldiers of the 254th were learning more about battle. My father writes on January 9, 1945, "I guess you might say we've been in combat. At least all our line companies have, and we've been under a little artillery fire." For those line companies, Harris Peel describes these first few weeks of January as a time when the expression "'as different as day and night' became a gross actuality."[31] He recounts the daytime hours as relatively pleasant; the men passed their time in cellars, where, although they were crowded, they had little to do but eat and sleep. However, "the night was filled with explosives and flares and magnified sounds. We sent patrols to infiltrate enemy lines; the Germans sent patrols to enter ours. . . . We saw men die and we realized how thin was the thread on which our lives dangled."[32]

For soldiers in the communications unit, like my father, there were different duties. Sergeant Lyle Atwood, my father's chief in the communications platoon at this point in the war, recalls them: "My job was to see to it that communications between our Infantry Companies and the others in our Battalion were connected. We did this by laying telephone lines between the Command Post and each company. The lines were connected to a switchboard at Headquarters Company and it was manned 24 hours a day. We also maintained radio contact with the Company Commanders and Battalion and Regiment and so on. . . . We also maintained a message center where we could decode all messages that came in from the enemy."[33] My father was involved in much of this work. He was assigned to the message center and sometimes worked the switchboard or the radio, though at this point he was most often used as a runner between units. He was happy, though, that he was not one of the men laying down wire. On January 19, he writes to his family that the "wire section is really having a rough time of it. Every day—usually in the afternoon—the lines are knocked out. So, when night comes, they have to go out & fix them. You see, some of our lines are laid in places where you can't go in the daytime—so the boys are up running around all night long."

It was also during this period that the 254th learned more about both allies and the enemy. The experienced 3rd Infantry Division, to which the 254th was attached, taught them much about soldiering in these first few weeks. Harris Peel wrote, "They never seemed to mind taking time to tell us about something we wished to know. If we became seasoned fighters in less time than the average regiment, it was probably due to the interest taken in us by this organization."[34] Other allies in this area included French Moroccan soldiers, who were very different from the typical American GI. As Carl Brass recalled, "All they wanted was a flashlight, a tommygun, and a knife. They patrolled the high ridges in the mountains and they were very treacherous. They were like cats. You couldn't hear them coming and you couldn't see them because they wore the white, and they were fierce fighters."[35]

Finally, it was during this time that members of the 254th realized they had caught the attention of the enemy. On January 21, members of the regiment received a pamphlet from the Nazis via leaflet shell, welcoming them to battle. The opening paragraph read:

> ***Soldiers of the Blood and Fire Division!!*** *We, the Krauts, salute. We're glad you've arrived! The idyllic days along the Mediterranean are over. You have come from the coast and antiaircraft, from training camp and other soft jobs where life was comparatively easy. But already camping in your tents you've learned that another breeze is blowing up here. It has not been exactly warm and comfortable, has it?*[36]

Though the soldiers may have chuckled about the "idyllic days along the Mediterranean" as they recalled the windswept rock that was Staging Area Number 2, this missive from Germany was a clear sign of difficult battles ahead. The first of these battles came for some members of the 254th on January 20, when orders came to take "Hill 216." This assignment involved the 1st and 3rd Battalions; my father's 2nd Battalion continued holding its defensive position. This was the first major offensive battle for the unit, and there were a number of casualties. In his unit history, Harris Peel boasts, "Tested in fire, the regiment proved that it could fight beside the veteran units of the famous 3rd Division. There was never a day after Hill 216 that our heads did not rise just a little higher when we said, 'I'm from the 254th Infantry.'"[37]

My father's onionskin list of locations records for January 25, 1945, "Arrived Illhaersern—Colmar Forest (Attacked Jebsheim France)." The next notation, for January 28, 1945, says, "Arrived Jebsheim France." In the few days encompassed by these notations, the Battle of Jebsheim took place, and these were among the toughest days experienced by the 254th. The Battle of Jebsheim came toward the end of the fighting in the Colmar Pocket. Jebsheim was one of the final villages held by the Germans in this area, was "a key north-south communications junction,"[38] and was thought to serve as German corps headquarters in the area. Unit histories recount the details of the battle as various companies approached the town from various angles, often met by fierce resistance from Germans holding buildings within the town or in dug-in positions around pillboxes. ("[Company] F passed through and led G," Peel writes, "which was to protect the left flank. E remained as battalion reserve in the defense positions occupied the night before by one of its platoons. Company C, with A following, launched the First Battalion's attack").[39]

The cold was particularly pronounced during these few days, leading to severe problems in the attack. "Weapons with bolts frozen refused to function in the freezing hands of their operators. Soon the weapons of other companies of each battalion failed to function for the same reason. With weapons that refused to fire the men found themselves practically helpless as they approached Jebsheim for the assault on the Maginot Line pillboxes protecting the town."[40]

Not surprisingly, my father did not find time to write any letters during these few days. Resuming his correspondence on January 29 (the final official day of the Battle of Jebsheim), he writes that "at present, we're living in a house in a small town. It's warm & comfortable." He also notes (with probable understatement) that "this is about the roughest we've had it since we've been here" and that "we've really been moving around quite a bit, from house to foxhole to barn." His retrospective notes in his diary from these days tell a somewhat more dangerous tale, though still a highly condensed one (for the practical reason that the diary was very small):

- *Thursday, Jan. 25, 1945: Left Ribeauville Station and went to woods. Dug a dugout and spent a long, wet, cold night. A few shells came in.*
- *Friday, January 26, 1945: Hassell and I got to the Barn (OP for Attack) this night. Phip and I went up in haymow. Toward morning terrible shelling. I was very scared. Jeep wrecked.*
- *Saturday, January 27, 1945: We went into Jebsheim late in the day—were shelled moderately on way in. One landed about 20 feet away.*
- *Sunday, January 28, 1945: At Jebsheim we at least had a house and stove. Still eating "C" rations—I had the G.I.'s and was pretty sick.*
- *Monday, January 29, 1945: We still got plenty of shelling at Jebsheim. Two "H" Co. runners were hurt when barn back of us was hit.*

Though soldiers in communications units were clearly not engaged in battle to the same extent as those in rifle companies (as my father says in his January 29 letter, "It's not too bad. A lot of poor guys have it worse"), the distinctions between soldiers in various roles undoubtedly blurred during the days of battle. When I asked Dad's buddy in the communications platoon, Carl Brass, about Brass's role during the Battle of Jebsheim, he told a story that may be representative of the activities of even "scrawny communications guys" during such operations:

The Captain, Captain Wright, took a liking to me, a little skinny kid. . . . Jebsheim was maybe two blocks long one direction and three blocks the other

> *direction. They were still fighting at the lower end of the street and Captain Wright told his orderly, like he always did, "Get Brass." So we went up in his jeep and we tried to get into Jebsheim. And it was so full of shell holes and the Germans were still shelling so we couldn't get in. So Captain Wright jumps out of the jeep and he starts running down the side of the road. And I'm saying this guy is fearless, or he doesn't have good sense. I had the most admiration for him. And 88s are heading all over. And he slips and falls on the ice and the snow was quite deep. So Tom Edge, his driver, was behind him and so was I. And we're laying on the ground and we thought, well, now he's got some sense, he's making the target as small as possible. And he gets up, and he says, I can still remember his words, he's mad as a hornet. He says "What the hell is the matter with you guys?" He says, "I slipped and fell on my ass and you two guys have to do the same thing!" So we made it all the way into town and we set up a forward OB [operating base] at the western edge of town that we used during that whole battle of Jebsheim.*[41]

By the end of January, Allied troops controlled the town of Jebsheim, in large part due to the efforts of the 254th Regiment of the 63rd Infantry Division. For their efforts in Jebsheim and earlier battles in the Colmar Pocket, units were presented a number of citations, including a Presidential Unit Citation for the entire regiment for Colmar Pocket, a Presidential Unit Citation for the 2nd Battalion for the Battle of Jebsheim, and the French Croix de Guerre with Palm. The 254th was praised in the glowing manner typical of such citations. From the Presidential Unit Citation for the 254th Infantry Regiment, 63rd Infantry Division, granted June 6, 1945:

> *Fighting incessantly, from 22 Jan to 6 Feb 1945, in heavy snow storms, through enemy infested marshes and woods and over a flat plain crisscrossed by numerous small canals, irrigation ditches, and unfordable streams, terrain ideally suited to the defense, [the 254th Infantry Regiment] breached the German defense wall on the northern perimeter of the Colmar bridgehead and drove forward to isolate Colmar from the Rhine.*

From the Presidential Unit Citation for the 2nd Battalion, 254th Infantry Regiment, granted May 7, 1946:

> *Slowly and grimly the men advanced, though suffering heavy casualties in the intense fire coming from three directions, took the concrete bunkers with the aid of tank destroyers and eliminated the resistance before the town which had*

> *previously turned back entire regiments. Penetrating the flaming town, the men fought bitterly against the desperate and determine[d] defender, neither giving nor asking quarter.*

And from the French Croix de Guerre with Palm citation, granted March 15, 1945:

> *[The regiment] captured during these actions, more than 4000 prisoners, thus concluding brilliantly the series of glorious operations which took place from the Mediterranean to the Rhine.*[42]

Paul Fussell has noted the inaccuracies of medal citations and argued that they "are the worst possible documents for historians to invoke for any purpose, except possibly satire."[43] Nevertheless, the somewhat melodramatic language of the citations and awards aside, the 254th performed admirably despite having been thrown into battle so quickly. They surprised not only themselves but, according to Peel, others as well: "It was not until later that we learned that the Third Division had not expected us to be able to capture [Jebsheim]. The question as to why our determination was so strong, our fighting so fierce, in taking this town was probably best answered by one Pfc who said, 'If you think I was going to stay out in some damn foxhole full of snow while the Krauts were living in nice, warm cellars, you're crazy!'"[44]

Toward, through, and beyond the Siegfried Line

> Conditions in the February fighting were different from January, yet just as miserable in their own way. . . . The first task was to get through the Siegfried line, still a formidable obstacle although in many places devoid of troops to utilize it. And every veteran in an ETO combat unit was well aware that this was where the Germans had stopped them in September 1944.
>
> STEPHEN E. AMBROSE, *Citizen Soldiers*

The Battle of Jebsheim ended in late January 1945, and the fight for positions in the Colmar Pocket continued into the first week in February. For the rest of February and into early March, the 254th Regiment worked its way north along towns and villages west of the Rhine. My father's location list reports arrivals in Enchenberg, Petit Rederching, St. Michel, Saargemines, and

Neunkirchen. The weather was not quite so severe, but it was still unpleasant. One soldier reported that "it was cold, but not quite cold enough to freeze, this February in 1945. Rain fell continually and things were in a muddy mess. Most of us were mud from head to foot, unshaven, tired and plagued by recurrent epidemic severe diarrhea."[45] A soldier from the 63rd Infantry described the fighting in February as "more of the same—another hill, another forest, another plan, another attack, and the inevitable counter-attack, and establishing strong defensive positions."[46]

For my father, however, conditions definitely improved during this time. In his diary and letters, he reports better living conditions at a French home, in an "insane asylum," and at a chateau. His work now mostly involved assignments with the radio division. He spent one day in four on patrol or at a forward dugout (described as "nice and cozy—low with a roof and a stove inside") manning the "300" radio. During the other three days, life was pretty easy. His letters describe buddies in his unit and their off-duty activities, ask his family for more letters and packages, and recount everyday encounters with some of the people in the villages. While in Enchenberg, members of the communications unit were housed in "a clean room in a clean house" with the French family still living below. On February 13 Dad writes,

> *The nicest people I've seen yet in France live in the same house with us, right downstairs. There is a boy about 12, a girl of 19 or 20, two older women, and one older man. It's now 11 o'clock at night—(I'm on telephone duty until 12)—& just got back from downstairs, where Phil, Boyd, Vaughan, I, & the kid were playing "parcheesi" and eating the girls' cookies. Really the first actual down-to-earth fun I've had in France. Andre—the kid—brings us a pitcher of good cold milk every night, and yesterday brought up a huge apple pie. That* really *was good.*

During this time the 254th was reunited with other regiments of the 63rd Infantry. Peel reports that the regiment as a whole was "feeling rather like a prodigal son who has left home, done well in the world and learned much, but is glad to be back."[47] This reunion with buddies from other units was a welcome one to Dad. He was particularly happy to see his good friend Harold West. On February 20 he writes to his parents from Saargemines, "At last, after almost two months, I've again met Harold. We found each other in this place. We sure had a swell time last night talking of our respective experiences and dreams of home." In all, these few weeks were a bit of a respite for the 254th. Though the regiment was still officially in battle, "maintaining defensive positions northeast of Sarreguimines and conducting extensive patrols and raids,"[48] there was time behind the line, and the soldiering took on a regular rhythm. For those in the communications units, life was particularly good. My father notes on February 28 in a letter from Neunkirchen, France, "I am feeling fine and dandy, our chow is good, & I get sufficient rest. In fact, I'd be content to remain here for the rest of the war."

Of course, it was not possible to remain in that relatively pleasant situation for the rest of the war. The march north from the Colmar Pocket was a move toward a final part of the German defense on the western front—the Siegfried line. The original Siegfried line was built by Germany in northern France during World War I. However, the Siegfried line that my father's unit was approaching was a defensive line built during the 1930s, opposite the French Maginot line. The Germans called it the Westwall. The line stretched for almost four hundred miles following the western border of the old German Empire from the border with the Netherlands to the border with Switzerland, and consisted of a series of bunkers with rounded lookouts on top (known as "pillboxes") and tank traps made of reinforced concrete (known as "dragon's teeth"). In a letter looking back on combat experiences several months later (May 25, 1945), my father describes the Siegfried line, and the actions of his unit, this way: "You want to know a little bit about the Siegfried line? I'm in a talkative mood today, so I'll tell you. It was composed of numerous huge concrete pillboxes dug into the ground, huge concrete Dragons Teeth set into the ground, communications trenches, and barbed wire. Our boys had to form into assault teams with dynamite wired to poles, and crawl up to the pillboxes and blast the occupants out. The engineers had to do the work on the Dragons Teeth, blasting them out so the tanks could roll through."

Throughout the struggle, Harris Peel reports, the soldiers kept their attention on their overriding purpose—to "[breach] the mighty Siegfried Line which Dr. Goebbels had described for so many years to the people of the world as 'Germany's impenetrable Westwall.'"[49] On March 13, according to my father's retrospective diary notes, the companies "were set up on defensive awaiting the big push. It came." Early on the morning of March 14, "after a terrific artillery barrage—one continuous roar—[the] 1st [Battalion] jumped off." As to my father's group, "We were in reserve and followed." By two o'clock the next morning, they had passed through Bluebransbach to Ensheim. "The Siegfried line was just in front of us."

Though the Siegfried line was, of course, attacked in multiple places along its four-hundred-mile span, the 63rd Infantry had orders to break through it in the sector near Ensheim. "The plan of attack," Peel observes, "had been skillfully prepared," and the three-part role of the 254th was clear: "First, the uncovering of the ground stretching before the Siegfried line by the First Battalion; second, the establishment and holding of a block by the Third Battalion; and third, the breaching of the Siegfried line by the Second Battalion assisted by the First."[50]

Dad was in the middle of the push for the line, which lasted from March 16 to March 20. With his twenty-five-pound SCT300 radio strapped to his back, he was out near the front with Colonel Warren, and he came under fire during all four days of the offensive. His diary entries are terse: on Friday, March 16, he writes, "Last two days rough. . . . We got beaucoup shells thrown at us." The next day he reports being "pinned down for half day by Jerry MG fire. Cos. having it rough cracking pillboxes and dragon's teeth." Then he was able to spend two nights back in town (Ensheim), "but rest of time during attack out in holes. Scared half to death the majority of time."

On March 19 the news in the diary is both good and bad: "Almost through the Siegfried—Cos. having high casualties. Jerries fighting like demons." And "still plenty shells." Then, on the 20th, he exhales: "Finally cracked it and pushed through to Oberwurtsbach. Sure a relief not to be attacking for a day or so."

But in writing home to his parents on March 22, Dad downplays the experience, noting that he had been "very busy" during the last few days and telling his parents, "since I wrote last I've been working with the 300 radio on my back quite a bit. I found it pretty unpleasant at times—it's a lot harder to dodge bullets and shells—but I always found consolation in the thought that the men on the line had it a lot worse."

James Hatcher points out in his memoir that the Siegfried line breakthrough of the 63rd Infantry was "the first to be achieved on the front of the Seventh Army or, for that matter, on the entire front of the Sixth Army Group.[51] For members of my father's unit, there was great pride in that accomplishment. Members of the division erected a sign: "You are now passing through the Siegfried Line courtesy 63d Infantry Division," which Marlene Dietrich posed beside when she came to entertain the troops a few days later on March 24. The 1st and 3rd Battalions of the 254th each received Presidential Unit Citations. James Hatcher took issue: "Why the 2nd Battalion, which had performed so brilliantly in its attack against the forts and pillboxes on the key terrain of Hill 333, was not cited is a matter I never have understood."[52] But, though his battalion as a whole was not given special recognition in this battle, Dad was. He was granted a Bronze Star. His citation reads, in part:

> *For four days he stayed at the battalion forward observation post, often in positions exposed to enemy mortar and artillery fire. Private First Class Miller's bravery and devotion to duty under hazardous conditions helped materially to maintain communication between the battalion observation post and the forward companies.*

The breakthrough at the Siegfried line occurred on March 20, 1945. It was exactly seven weeks before V-E Day and five weeks and three days before the 254th was relieved from active duty and pulled to a back line position (on April 27). The war in Europe was clearly in its final throes—the Russians were marching westward through Eastern Germany toward Berlin, and other Allied troops were progressing eastward toward Berlin and southward toward the Danube. But Hitler reacted to setbacks on all fronts with increasing desperation. "In a drastic scorched earth policy [he] ordered the destruction of anything the Allies might find of value"; he threw barely trained recruits into battle and "ordered the summary execution of any soldier who displayed defeatism by advocating surrender or retreat"; and he instituted a "total war" policy in which the entire German population was exhorted to fight guerilla style as the Allies advanced through their towns and villages.[53] Few Germans followed this edict, but clearly the end of the war in Europe was not going to come easily.

The path of my father's unit during this time was first eastward across the Rhine at Mannheim and then south in a push toward the Danube through villages such as Sindolsheim, Krautheim, Dorrenzimmern, Kunselsau, Gottwollshaunsen, Schwabish Hall, Unter-Aspach, and Gertstetten. His unit crossed the Rhine on March 28 as part of the crossing of the U.S. Seventh Army between Mannheim and Worms. Almost a month later, on April 25, the unit crossed the Danube and arrived in Leipsheim. The path between the Rhine and the Danube was a bloody one for the 63rd Infantry—the division sustained more combat deaths in April 1945 than in any other month (221 killed in action compared to 117 in March, 76 in February, and 90 in January).[54] Peel notes that while headlines in the U.S. were screaming about a "complete rout," the 254th Regiment received more than six hundred replacements.[55] The battles during this time were particularly difficult because the situation was so fluid: "There were no more definite German lines just as there were no longer any static friendly ones."[56] Thus, units would approach a town or village not knowing exactly what to expect, clear it out, perhaps bed down for the night, then move on through the forests—sometimes stopping in foxholes—toward the next village. On April 8, Dad reports in the diary, "Left Merchingen and really took off. Didn't stop for three weeks. I started out with the Colonel." The diary for the next few weeks bristles with entries like "shoved off on attack"; "off again on rugged attack"; "more attack—still motorized"; "more attack, met pretty rough artillery fire, rained, miserable day"; "very rough day. Walked about 25 miles. Had Kraut carrying radio last 5 miles"; "still going"; "still shoving on," until finally—on April 27—he records, "Bn. relieved. Late in afternoon took off for the rear."

But whatever the diary says, Dad's letters home refer to the perils and struggles of war only obliquely. On April 2 he tells his folks that "we have been on the move, and have lived in the woods. . . . It was a little rough." On April 6 he writes, "You should be able to gather that we have not been idling about in a defensive situation. Disbrow and myself have been traipsing around the countryside with a 300 radio providing communications for the colonel. It was a pretty hectic assignment in many ways." On April 18 he does report a death in the communications platoon: "One of my buddies—Harry Kaufman (I may have mentioned him in my letters before) got it yesterday. A sniper got him in the back. Harry was born in this neighborhood of Germany & was ace interpreter of the battalion."

But in general Dad's letters do not concentrate on the ongoing attacks. He talks with surprise about the amenities of the homes in the towns and villages, a reaction apparently shared by many GIs. One private, Joe Burns, recalled a wondrous opportunity to enjoy a hot shower: "Fifty-one years later he declared it to be 'the most exquisite five minutes of [his] life.'"[57] There was also often better food now, as soldiers found provisions in the homes and supplemented them with cognac and wine that they found in the cellars. On March 27, just before crossing the Rhine, Dad describes the improvement in comestibles: "Even the kitchen can't spoil our fun by serving K rations occasionally. We just up and cook our own food. For instance—this noon we had corn, peas and carrots, and fried potatoes, topped off by some delicious canned cherries. All through the courtesy of the departed Nazis. The other night we had French Fried chicken, French fried potatoes, champagne to wash it down with."

In these final weeks of the war, then, the continuing stress of battle was mitigated by the pleasures of time spent with buddies enjoying better living conditions in German villages, and by the realization that the war was coming to an end. But that it wasn't coming any faster was clearly frustrating. On April 26, the day before his unit was pulled off the front line, Dad wrote, "Well, the Russians finally hit Berlin, but the war still drags on and on. People in the States say the war is nearly over, over here & appear very optimistic. Perhaps they are right—but they don't realize that every second the war drags on might mean life or death to some poor rifleman."

Then, a few weeks later, the war in Europe finally ran down. My father's diary entry on May 1 reads, "Saw movie tonight—old but good. . . . Hot news. Hitler dead." Two days later he writes home, "Looks like the war is going to end any minute over here. Just heard the news over the radio. Very encouraging." And two days after this, in his final letter before V-E Day, he writes, "Something is 'up.' It has to be. We're just being treated too good recently." Something was up. My father's time in war was over.

Unfortunately, his time in Europe wouldn't end for almost eleven months.

Waiting to Go Home

> Don't write home and tell your mother or sweetheart that you'll be home next week or next month. For most of you, it just ain't so.
>
> DON WILLIAMS, *Stars and Stripes*

The "Blood and Fire" 63rd Infantry Division had been activated on June 15, 1943, and spent 119 days in combat between December 1944 and April 1945. Its World War II battle credits include Alsace, Saar, the Siegfrield line, the Rhineland, Württemberg, and Bavaria. Peel reports that "On June 15, 1945, just two years after our activation, we received the word that the Regiment had completed its work; it was to go back to the United States for deactivation."[58] Members of the division began going home on August 21, 1945, and deactivation of the 63rd became official on September 27, 1945. But the deactivation of the division did not mean that all—or even most—of the soldiers in the division were discharged. Indeed, most of them had a long wait, as on May 12, 1945, the military instituted a "point system" to guide the demobilization process. According to this plan, soldiers were awarded points based on the number of months they had spent in the army since September 16, 1940, the number of months they had spent overseas, the number and type of decorations they had won in combat, and the number of children they had under the age of eighteen. Soldiers with more points would be the first in line for discharge. President Truman defended the system in a speech on June 1, 1945:

> *The Army's system for selecting the soldiers for release to civilian life represents a democratic and fair approach to this most difficult problem. A poll was*

> *taken among enlisted men in all parts of the world. They were asked what factors they believed should be taken into consideration in deciding who should be released from the Army first. More than 90 percent said that preference should go to those who had been overseas and in combat longest, and to those with children. . . . The system applies equally to the members of our Army in all parts of the world. It embodies the principles of impartial selection that we applied in drafting our citizen Army and that we shall continue to apply in meeting the manpower requirements of our armed forces until Japan is defeated.*[59]

Soldiers in Europe were apparently cognizant of the point system within days of its announcement. On May 12, my father writes home that "nobody can do anything but guess as to what we are going to do or when. The point system doesn't work out very well for me or the rest of the guys who are my buddies. I have exactly 28 points, whereas 85 are needed at present for possible discharge. I guess I'm doomed to stay in for a while longer." His point total was destined to go up as he stayed overseas longer and as battle awards were bestowed. By May 31 he could write home of his "magnificent total of 37—almost half of what is required," and by the time of his discharge, he had 45 points. Regardless of the precise total, though, the point system assured that my father—along with most other soldiers in Europe—would not leave the military soon.

Knowing they were not leaving the army did little to relieve soldiers' uncertainty about what the future held. Even before European hostilities ended in early May, rumors were flying about what would happen next. There were a number of possibilities: being shipped directly to the PTO (Pacific Theater of Operations) or CBI (China—Burma—India); being shipped to the PTO via the United States; being reassigned to a unit within the United States; or staying on in Europe. Early rumors made my father think going to the Pacific was likely (May 25: "Will we or won't we get furloughs in the States before we hit CBI? I certainly hope they route us through the USA"), and he became more sure of this after he learned of the deactivation of his unit. On June 18, he writes,

> *The 63rd Division is being split up. We'll all be shipped to other Class II Divisions over here to fill in. By Class II is meant a division going to the Pacific* via *the States. I warn you now, I may end up in a rifle company in some other outfit—or I may get a good break and end up in a headquarters outfit. When I'll get shipped I don't know. I think I can safely say that I'll be in the States late*

this summer or early fall. Get it out of your heads that I'm going to be in the army of occupation, because I'm not. As Uncle Louie (Gen. Hibbs) would say, "I'm a combat soldier."

The uncertainty and the rumors continued through the rest of June and July. There was the rumor that all the men would be kept in the division, meaning that my father would be home later in the year. But there were also rumors that his current classification as clerk-typist had been deemed "essential," meaning that his return would be delayed. He was joined by his buddies in his uncertainty and nervousness about the future. On June 27 he writes, "The boys around here have a new saying which characterizes the suspense and anxiety they are going through now—you know, sweating out getting in a headquarters company in some good division. It's 'Are you nervous in the service? Are you fed up with the set up? Are you crackin' up from the shakin' up?'"

There were major changes for my father on the home front. His father died on June 19, although Dad didn't learn this news for more than a week. An analysis of the effect of this event on him follows in chapter 3's discussion of family relationships. However, it is noteworthy that my grandfather died during the hubbub regarding who would go where, and one possible result of this is that Dad was not given a furlough to go home following his father's death. However, he did get a leave to Paris in early July, from which he returned in mid-July to continue the uncertain wait. He took some solace in war news from the Pacific (July 15: "I see by the paper today that they've got the fleet shelling Japan proper now. . . . Maybe by the time they decide to ship this outfit out of the ETO the Japanese war will be almost over"). He also continued with his desultory clerical duties and with a bit of soldiering (July 21: "Had a big search of houses and people today, rounding up all pro-Nazis"). But it wasn't until the end of July that he learned more about his future in the army.

On August 3, he writes his family that he is back in Paris, "on temporary loan to the Command Schools branch of the Information and Education Division of Theater Service Forces." He was billeted at a Paris art museum—the Petit Palais. This beautiful museum is in operation today, holding a variety of collections, but in 1945 it was transformed by bunks in all the galleries, a dayroom, and a tailor and a barber shop. On a trip to Paris with my mother in the 1980s, Dad could point out the spot in the museum where his bunk had stood. In 1945, though, his principal interest in the museum was its proximity to the Red Cross Club across the street and to theaters and nearby cafés, which offered a decided improvement over typical army fare. His work in Paris was a happy change from his life in wartime, as he explains to his mother on August 3:

> *I go to work at 0830 in the morning, get from 12 to 1 for lunch, and work till 5:30 in the afternoon. The rest of my time is free. We get Sundays off, and will get one afternoon per week off in addition, whenever I get attached to the right place. The work isn't hard, although it's hard to catch on at first, as there are so many complicated forms of correspondence. The surroundings are pleasant. I am working at present in an office on the second floor of a building about a block off the Arc De Triomphe.*

Dad stayed in Paris through the month of August and into September. He went into the hospital with a foot infection, and when he came out, the war was over: "As the French headlines screamed yesterday, 'La guerre est fini.' And a huge Stars and Stripes banner contained just one word—'PEACE.' I am really thankful it is finally finished, because of all the boys in the Pacific. The effect on my status is negligible right at the present time."

Dad's life developed a comfortable rhythm of work during the day, shows or other social activities on nights and weekends, writing long (though less frequent) letters home, and obsessing over the point system (September 8: "You may think it strange that in practically every letter I mention something about points and chances of getting home in the future. That is just about all anyone over here ever talks about"). The routine didn't change greatly when his job, and along with it his quarters, moved from Paris to Versailles, just a short walk from the summer palace of French kings, on September 16. Some of the facilities were inferior to those at the Petit Palais, but the food was great, and Dad maintained the same work schedule and had the same freedom to come and go at will. He made many trips to Paris, both for work and play, and continued his duties of typing, cataloguing, and procuring.

The routine was varied somewhat by his interest in the array of post-war opportunities to make some extra cash. On September 3 he writes,

> *Looked at some stamps of Peel's this morning that he picked up in Germany (a whole album of them) and is going to try to sell. If he gets a good price for them, and he should inasmuch as prices are so inflated in Paris at the present time, I am going to ask you to send my collection over here (it is better than the one Peel has) and sell it and send you the money. But don't do anything yet. Boy, with the right kind of goods over here, a man could make a fortune in a very short time. And some of the higher ups are making fortunes, too.*

I don't think he ever sold his stamp collection following this initial flare of interest, but he did start dealing in some other goods (October 18: "Sold three cartons of cigarettes yesterday for 40 bucks—or rather Miss Sadik, a civilian clerk in the administrative office, sold them for me for 45 bucks of which I took 40"). Some of the money he made was sent home, and some was used to fund activities in Paris and a weekend leave to Brussels. In November, he and his friend Cy Field started planning a road trip through the American and Canadian West for the summer months after their anticipated discharge in 1946, so more money was needed. He writes on November 26,

> *Well, Cy and I have some of the money details of our trip planned. I now have four watches to sell, about 30 bars of candy, and about 15 bars of soap. The watches are some Wally Holland brought back from Switzerland for us, and that one you sent me. I am going to sell all that stuff and send the dough to Cy some way or another. Haven't quite figured out a way to do it. That should net us something close to 175 bucks which will pay all our gasoline and automobile costs. Then Cy is going to send me beaucoups cigarettes when he gets home which I will proceed to sell and send him the money. All this will go into a little fund marked "trip." Then when next summer rolls around there won't be too much expense involved. That is, all this is tentative, depending on whether or not you approve of my taking this little journey.*

And so it went through the rest of 1945. In the middle of December, Dad was transferred to a new post with the Information and Education Division in Höscht, Germany, just outside Frankfurt. But before he got settled there, a furlough to London finally came through. He went back to Paris to pick up all the paperwork, waited for transport to London on Christmas Eve, and spent the holidays in England, seeing all the sights and thinking of home. As the end of 1945 approached, he worked to get a call through to Urbana and looked back on the year that had passed. On December 30, 1945, he writes, "Let's see, where was I last New Year's. Wait'll I look it up in my pocket itinerary. Oh yes, we got to Diefenbach, France, on Dec. 31 and spent New Year's Eve there. As I recall, I slept on a table in a café that night. Dern town was too small to even house our company comfortably. We pulled out the next day, anyway."

As 1946 began, my father returned to Höchst to the regular routine (January 12, 1946: "Things around here are about the same as when I left—very little work to do, and nobody doing that"). By this time, though, he clearly believed that he would be home in a matter of a few months. He continued to follow the news about the point system and discharges in the *Stars and Stripes*, sometimes grousing about favorable treatment given to other branches of the military. On January 12 he argues, "I fully realize that men are needed over here to occupy Germany, but I also know that a lot of air corps cadets and other guys in other branches have been discharged in the States with less than 20 points." A few days later, though, he was celebrating a "definite statement from the war department" that led him to believe he would be back in the States by late April or early May. There were rumors floating around in the local bar for servicemen ("The Low Pointer's Inn"), and, because Dad was working in a clerical role, he could track the points of those being discharged. On March 16, he writes home that Dick Carr—a 46-pointer—got his orders. So Dad, a 45-pointer—knew that "at long last the time has come—or rather will come in a few days."

Four days later, he was in the office to take the call himself: "Boy, I was sitting in the office today typing out some stuff for Peel, when the phone rings. 'AG Art Section.' 'You have a Sergeant Brisbon, Cpl. Miller and Pfc. Van Vliet in that Section?' 'Sure do.' 'Well, tell them to come to Frankfurt this afternoon to pick up their redeployment orders. Room 021A, IG Farben Bldg.' Yipe. What a lovely sound."

A few hours later, he sat down at the typewriter to compose one of his final letters home. The closing of the letter is the typical, "As always, Love, Bud." But the opening of the letter is something he'd been waiting to write for a long time:

Dear Mom and all,

Break out the flags and Pepsi-Cola Mom, your Son is coming home.

Family and Fatherhood

> While I was still in the army, he died. On my emergency furlough, I saw him that last day at County Hospital. His last words were, "Boy, you're the man of the house now. You gotta take care of your mother." . . . Those four years in the army are the turning point in my life. I learned something about men. . . . I learned something about myself.
>
> DEMPSEY TRAVIS, IN STUDS TERKEL'S *The Good War*

THE TRANSFORMATION TO ADULT LIFE happens across a variety of contexts—in work, with friends, in romance, at school, in public life. But because the family is one of the most formative and central institutions in society, the transition to adulthood in the family context is particularly crucial. Family roles and expectations for behavior change as an individual advances through infancy, childhood, and adolescence into adulthood, growing increasingly more independent. These changes in roles and expectations make themselves felt in other areas of life as well. Taking on the role of "father," for instance, has implications for work and friendship. Thus, in this first analytical chapter considering the ways in which my father's experiences in World War II influenced his transition from boy to man, I consider his relationships with members of his family and how those relationships were transformed both through his experiences in the war and through his father's death in June 1945 while Dad was still stationed in Europe.

My father undoubtedly would have agreed about the importance of family during this period of his life. Early in his basic training at Camp Blanding, he asked for photographs of his father, mother, and sister Judy, and on March 30, 1944, he wrote, "Gee, I look at those pix of you every chance I get. Boy you sure look beautiful, Mom. And Dad—such a handsome man." His thoughts of family helped my father get through rough bouts of homesickness at Camp Van Dorn: "I have made up my mind to just live through this rotten war as best I can—for I *know* better & happier days are ahead for all of us. Like you said, Mom, *we* are the only people who count" (July 19, 1944). And, at the end of his final furlough before being shipped overseas, he talks about how his love of family is related to his role in the war effort, itself: "I feel mighty lucky to have parents such as you folks are. If I ever have to go into the actual war (as I *don't* think I'll have to), you folks will be *what I'm* fighting for. (Does that sound mushy? Well, it's true, nevertheless)" (October 21, 1944).

As he left for basic training, my father's role in the family was fixed and firm. He was the only son, and he had a relationship with his father centered in the male activities of hunting, fishing, and sports. His relationship with his mother was respectful and loving, but it also involved some teasing (about, for instance, her false teeth and her attempts at art and creative writing). He saw his relationship with his older sister, Dorothy ("Sis"), as one of relative equality, and they often shared opinions about books, movies, and music. He was a big brother to his sister Judy, asking about her activities at camp, giving her advice about high school, and commenting on her move into adolescence (on receiving a photo on March 26, 1944, he writes, "Your looks have really improved since I left, Judy. You are quite a gal").

A year later, after fifteen months in the army and experiences in some of the roughest battles of the northwestern European campaigns, little of this had changed. Dad still saw his family as the central aspect of his life and his position as *son,* his most important role. On April 2, 1945, he writes, "The more I reflect upon it and think about it, the more I believe that this war and the army life is just a passing interlude, a mere incident in the life I was intended—and want—to live. I have—and want you to have—great faith in the belief that within the next year or possibly even less I will once more be home as a civilian, student, reporter, and above all, son."

And, at the end of that month, he meditates on his desire to resume boyhood when he returns home: "It seems strange to me to be called a man, for in my mind I still act like a boy—yet, I am doing a man's work—I can't reconcile myself to that fact. Perhaps it's because when I left home I *was* a boy—and for me life ceased at that point—to be resumed once again when I return home" (April 29).

This longed-for return to an idyllic childhood would probably never have happened in any event, but it became impossible when Dad's father died less than two months later, on June 19, 1945. My father's relationships with his mother and younger sister clearly shifted at this point, because although he was still a son, he also became the "man of the family," and he felt responsible for many aspects of its well-being. In this chapter, then, I will consider my grandfather's death as a turning point in the family journey my father took from boyhood to manhood.[1] In the first section I will examine the ways in which his letters home are representative of his boyhood identity. Then I will take up my grandfather's unexpected death while my father participated in mopping-up activities in postwar Germany. Finally, I will look first at the ways in which the content and tone of Dad's letters changed after his father's death, and then at several cultural, sociological, and psychological explanations for these changes.

Bud as Boy

In his stateside letters home during basic training, my father's letters to his parents served both as a reflection *of* his childhood and as a means of reflecting *on* his childhood. His correspondence was a reflection *of* his childhood in the sense that he spoke often of the activities and concerns that were central for him during his first eighteen years, including hunting, fishing, sports, and everyday family life. His letters, though, did more than provide this descriptive link, as he also became self-reflexive in considering his childhood and adolescence. In these reflections *on* his early life, he talked about how his new experiences gave him a fresh appreciation for his parents, his family, and his life in small-town Illinois.

REFLECTIONS OF CHILDHOOD

As noted in chapter 1, my father's childhood was in many ways typical of that of boys growing up in small midwestern towns during the Great Depression. There were family worries about employment and about economic hardship, but these concerns were of relatively minor importance to children. What had mattered to my father as a child and adolescent were the sports fandom and hunting and fishing that he shared with his father. In basic training, he continued to connect with these most pleasurable aspects of his childhood. His work with firearms provided a link back to his father and hunting, and his experiences in new parts of the country were a constant reminder of his favorite fishing holes near Urbana:

> MARCH 5, 1944: *By the way, Dad, I think you'd really love that carbine we fired Saturday. The thing is a powerful .30 caliber up to 600 yards. It is real light—5 pounds—has very little kick, and is semi-automatic, just keep pulling the trigger. An ideal deer rifle, one of the boys told me.*

> APRIL 2, 1944: *Of course, no fishing is allowed, but, Dad, I saw some of the largest catfish & bass in that Silver River I have ever seen. And perch—they swarm all over the place. We had some popcorn—all you do is hold a grain in your fingers, & a perch will come right up & jump for it.... In spots, though, the river made me very homesick. I could have sworn, at times, I was downriver from the bridge at Rocky Ford on the Saltfork.*

The references to hunting and fishing even continued in letters from just behind the lines in Europe. In a letter from "somewhere in France" sent on February 1, 1945, Dad writes, "I'll wager the streams around here are full of fish.... I'd certainly love to cast a plug over some of these French waters." And, in the same letter: "You should be over here, Dad, to go hunting. Great, huge rabbits play in the fields in groups of 5 & 6. I've shot at several, but missed." He also reported on other soldiers who did not miss—indeed, the wildlife of Northern Europe that winter was probably no match for the firepower of the Allied forces. Dad reported on several animals being cut down by machine gun fire, including a chicken and young deer.

My father's interest in sports also persisted in the military. Like hunting and fishing, following his favorite teams provided an ongoing link to his childhood and his father. He tried to follow the local Illinois teams and was always concerned about getting his hometown *News-Gazette.* He was especially sad during the springtime when he missed his favorite high school sporting event, the state basketball tournament. On March 12, 1944, during his first spring away, he writes from Camp Blanding, "Well, next week is state tournament week. Sure wish I could be there. I trust you'll listen to it all." Exactly one year later, he is still fondly remembering his days watching basketball:

> *The News-Gazette has begun to arrive regularly. Certainly wish I were back with the boys—*especially *today, as I notice the state tournament opens today. I certainly hate to miss this most enjoyable sports event of the year. From what I've read in the papers, Champaign has a good team this year—hope they go a long way toward victory. I can hardly realize that this year will be the second tourney in a row I've missed. The whole scene—gym, crowd, press-box, and teams—seems so crystal clear in my mind's eye. It's hard for me to believe that I'm starting my second year in the service.*

And Dad stayed interested in the national sports scene, too, especially baseball. He grew up cheering for the Chicago Cubs (and, to his lasting frustration, remained a fan throughout his life), and his father was a fan of both the Cubs and the American League St. Louis Browns. During the summer of 1944, when many major league players were serving in the military, the baseball world was without most of its stars, but my father still followed the sport voraciously. Early in the season, on April 20, he writes his father, "See the Cubs have dropped 2 out of 3 to Cincy. The usual Cub start, I suppose, Dad. Say, your Browns are really doing alright! 3 straight—they're headed for the World Series." A few weeks later, on May 7, he writes, "Sure looks like the Browns are on top to stay, Dad. At least I hope so. Don't worry about the Cubs. They'll win the pennant yet." Dad's prognostications proved true for the Browns—in spite of stiff competition from the Detroit Tigers, they won the only pennant in their history. His Cubs, however, didn't come close in the National League pennant race.

The next year, my father was still the unflagging Cubs supporter. And in that summer of 1945, again with many major leaguers still overseas, the Cubs came through and won the pennant, three games ahead of the St. Louis Cardinals. They met the Detroit Tigers in the World Series—a series described by Chicago sportswriter Warren Brown as the "World's Worst Series."[2] But this kind of negative thinking was not part of Dad's world, as he eagerly followed the back-and-forth events of the fall classic. On October 10, 1945, he writes, "Peel and I listened to the sixth game of the series Monday night—had quite a lot of excitement—you know he is for the Tigers and I for the Cubs. The big final game is tonight and we both plan to be right beside the radio during the entire game." Of course, a win was not in the offing for the Cubs, and my father was again disappointed. But his ongoing love of sport provided an important connection to home and family throughout his military service.

Finally, my father's letters home were reflections *of* his childhood in their descriptions of everyday life. He felt an important connection to home when a box from Oscar's print shop arrived on February 11, 1944: "Like my classy stationery? The best printer (and Dad) in the world printed it for me, & I don't doubt that the best embosser (and Mom) embossed it. This paper makes me the envy of hut number seven." He also thought about the daily rhythms of life at home, especially as they pertained to food. Early letters often provided menu information (on February 27, 1944: "For chow at noon we had roast turkey—I got a lot of white meat—peas, mashed potatoes, slaw, dressing, coffee, bread & butter, & ice cream"), and he was especially ebullient when the food reminded him of home. For example, a letter sent March 5, 1944, gives the details of an off-base meal with a buddy and his cousins: "If I wasn't sure I was in Florida, I'd have sworn that dinner came from the wonderful hands of the best cook in the world—you, Mom. We had roast beef, just like you fix it. Potatoes & carrots together—you know how you do it. Salad, with avocadoes. Graham cracker pie. HOT ROLLS—(HIGH ONES) WITH PLENTY OF BUTTER AND JELLY." While in Europe, he continued to comment extensively on what he ate, and to request food that reminded him of his childhood (like pimento cheese and Fanny Farmer candy).

He also found reflections of his family in the people of Europe. On February 23, 1945, in the midst of the push between the Colmar Pocket and the Siegfried Line, he writes from a village in France, "Today was a beautiful day, reminiscent of spring. It was delightful just watching the kids around here play—hopscotch, jump the rope, & the games the kids at home play. The only difference is the language they shout in. There was one little group playing right near the house. Two girls, a boy, & a little fellow about Andy's size. Sure reminded me of Andy, too—trying to join in the fun of the older ones—emulating them in all they'd do."

REFLECTIONS ON CHILDHOOD

In addition to these reflections *of* his childhood, my father's letters were also clearly reflections *on* his childhood. During basic training, Dad lived and worked with people quite different from those he had known as a child, and his letters were filled with reflexive ruminations on how he had been raised, and sometimes on how he was changing. These musings began in early letters at the start of basic training, like one written on February 4, 1944:

> *This army is teaching me many habits, some good some bad. I take a shower every night, I drink one or two cups of coffee per meal (I'm getting to like it, Dad), but worst of all I now swear occasionally. At the chow table, you just about have to do it in order to get salt or butter or bread passed to you. It's a funny thing, but I never appreciated all the fine things my Dad and Mom have done for me until now. After seeing some of the uncouth characters around here, I am sure glad I had Mr. & Mrs. O.F. Miller to bring me up correctly.*

His reflections on and longing for home in Urbana became particularly poignant when he was homesick. On April 24, 1944, he writes, "Boy, I'm really homesick this week. Don't know what's wrong, but everything I see or do reminds me of home. The thing I think of most is a meal of beans & biscuits at home on a Tues. nite, then sitting in the living room listening to Fibber McGee with you folks—no one else, just us." And though the homesickness abated when he was overseas, his reflections on the "good old days" did not, and he put these longings into the context of the war effort. Early in his days in France, on January 9, 1945, he writes,

> *I think of home practically all the time I'm not busy. But, peculiarly, I don't get homesick. Most of the time I reflect warmly about the life I led as a civilian. How you, Dad, used to willingly give me the car on Sunday night to go to a show with J.J.P.—about a nice, warm bath, dressing up in my good suit—picking up John—returning home at 12 or 1 o'clock & tossing the keys on the table downstairs. And, naturally, as every other doughboy does, I dream of a soft bed, a hot shower, plenty of good food, Pepsi-Cola—and mostly you folks, the ones I love most in this screwed-up world.*

As he reflected on his family and on his life as a child and an adolescent, Dad thought particularly of his mother and father. In his first year away from home in 1944, significant holidays and birthdays, especially, led him to think about the value of his parents and of the everyday pleasures of life before the army. On May 14, 1944, he writes to his mother alone:

> *Yes, today is Mother's Day—your day. All day Cal's radio has been playing sentimental songs about home & Mother. And here I am 1000 miles from home.*
>
> *Well, maybe in 3 or 4 more weeks I'll be home for a short time. At least I certainly hope so. You want to know what I want to do at home?*
>
> *Well, I want to get up late, sit in the living room & drink Pepsi with you for breakfast. Just like we used to do on Sundays. I want to see you all spruced up, like Dad described in one of his letters. And I'd also like to see you in that condition lacking teeth & combed hair.*
>
> *In fact, all I want is everything the way it was before I left.*
>
> *"Absence makes the heart grow fonder." Certainly a true saying for me. I remember how I used to argue about inconsequential things. I never did think about everything you & Dad did for me. I certainly think of them now, though.*

Then, later that summer, in the oppressive heat of Camp Van Dorn, he wrote a letter to his father on July 29 to honor his fifty-fourth birthday. The entire letter is included here:

Dear Dad,

HAPPY BIRTHDAY!!! I hope this reaches you on Monday in time for your birthday. A little token of my esteem was routed through Chicago to you.[3] *I hope* that *reaches you in time too. Birthday cards are scarce around here, so I'm letting this letter act as a birthday card to you.*

You know, Dad if I can only be as good a man as you are someday, I'll consider myself a success in this world—because with me YOU'RE a tremendous success. I hope I've lived up to your expectations as a son. I know I'm no good as a soldier, but I hope you still consider me o.k. as a son. This is the first—and last, I hope—time I've missed being home for your birthday. In 1945 we'll go fishing TOGETHER on your birthday. At present you are right in the prime of life, with many more happy birthdays ahead of you.

Well, you can get the news from the family letter—just consider this a little personal greeting from your ever-loving son.

Sadly, my grandfather died about a month before that next birthday, while Dad was participating in operations in Germany following the end of the war in Europe. Many rites of passage can mark the transition from boy to man. One of those is participation in a war. Another is the death of a parent. Thus, it is not at all surprising that the boyhood recollections in my father's letters home largely stopped in the summer of 1945. He had become the "man of the family," and he set aside the concerns of childhood and adolescence.

A Death in the Family

My grandfather, Oscar Francis Miller, died on June 19, 1945. The cause of death was heart failure, though it is not clear if there was a sudden heart attack or if there had been a more prolonged struggle with congestive heart problems. His death was unexpected, though he had been feeling ill and was having continuing dental problems. My father commented many times in his letters about these issues (on June 21, 1945: "Say, Dad, I want you to get these teeth in. Gee, I don't want to come home to a 'toothless' Dad. Besides, I know you'll look and feel a lot better when you have your false teeth"). It is possible that his dental problems contributed to my grandfather's death; research during the last few decades has found a consistent link between tooth and gum disease and the risk of both chronic and acute cardiovascular disease.[4] My aunt also suggested that stress might have contributed to the heart ailment:

"He was so worried about, you know, Joe being overseas and everything, and taking care of the rest of the family and all of that. I think it just got to him."[5] Whether the major contributing factor was periodontal disease or the stresses of wartime America, the fact is that my grandfather was laid to rest on June 21, 1945, at a cemetery near his boyhood home of Oakwood, Illinois. His obituary notes that "the deceased was born in Oakwood, on July 31, 1890, the son of the late Mr. and Mrs. Andrew Miller. He grew to manhood there and learned the printer's trade when a young man. . . . He is survived by his wife, Mrs. Irene Miller and two daughters and a son; Mrs. Dorothy Benner of Urbana; Miss Judith Miller at home and Pfc. Joe Ted Miller with the American forces in Germany."

My father did not know about his father's death until at least a week after the funeral. I am not sure whether he was informed by letter, telegram, or a phone call, but however the news came, it must have been a blow.[6] Half a world away from his mother and sisters, he must have felt stunned and stricken and isolated. There was no opportunity for a bereavement leave. He had been planning a leave to Paris; he took it, and his friend Bob Nielsen went with him. Interestingly, there was little comment on or processing of his father's death in Dad's letters home immediately after he learned the news, and what there was, was oblique. For instance, on July 7, 1945, while he was in Paris: "And there are a lot of pipe stores. If Dad were still with us, I'd certainly have purchased one for him. Gee, I know Dad would have loved to hear about Paris."

I did find one letter from this time that spoke directly to my grandfather's death, but it was written to Argyle Hauser, a minister and friend of Oscar's who was serving as a chaplain in the Pacific. When he got the letter, Reverend Hauser sent it along to Dad's mother with a note that began, "Yours is a great son indeed!" My grandmother kept it with all my father's letters. The letter to Reverend Hauser, written on July 14, 1945, reads, in part:

> *Wherever you may be, though, I'm sure you have heard of my dear Father's death. I'm also sure that you mourn his passing almost as much as myself. You were one of the best friends Dad ever had—I'm sure, if it had been possible, he would have liked for you to be the Reverend at his funeral.*
>
> *The news was a great shock to me. I knew Dad was not in good health, but I believed that after his teeth were removed he would regain his health in a short time. Thank God, he did not suffer any pain in passing. I'm positive that Heaven is one good soul richer at this time. It's hard for some to realize, but the* real *life is, after all, the after life. That's what* really *counts.*

These comments are somewhat surprising, given the atheism my father professed for most of his life. Perhaps he was just providing an account that would be pleasing to "old Argyle," or perhaps he was trying on a more spiritual identity for size. Or he could have been looking for a way to comfort himself and assuage whatever guilt he may have felt about his own involvement in his father's death. These feelings became clear in the one letter he wrote home—two weeks later—that expressed shared mourning with his mother and sisters:

> *And I feel the army has robbed me—and you folks, too—of what could have been some of the happiest months of my life. And, worst of all, I was robbed of the last few months of my Dad's life. Perhaps if I hadn't come overseas Dad wouldn't have suffered a heart stroke. Or perhaps it was me that did it. As I look back, I realize with a pang that some of my letters written in the stress of combat might very possibly have caused worry on his part. All my love is now concentrated in a small bundle and includes my mom, my sisters, my b.-in-law, and my nephews.*

Clearly, then, my father suffered in thinking about his father's death and deeply regretted being so far away from his family. However, his letters do not suggest that he wallowed in these emotions. Instead, his correspondence during the rest of his months in Europe evidenced a major shift in content and tone as he took on the mantle of "man of the family."

Bud as Man

It is not surprising that the letters my father wrote home after June 1945 were different from those he had written earlier. After all, the war in Europe was over, and he was leading a very different life—one of settled day-to-day work and leisure in Germany, Paris, or Versailles, as opposed to one of tramping through frigid countryside in the mud and the snow with a radio strapped to his back. However, there were more changes in my father's correspondence than just the nature of the activities he reported on; his letters from July 1945 through March 1946 show a marked shift in both content and tone as he adjusted to a new relationship with his mother and his sisters and to new ideas about who he was as the surviving male member of his family.

One change was in his greater attention to the practical and economic details of life. He was concerned about what would become of the print shop and his father's other possessions. On July 15, 1945, he writes, "By the way, what do you plan on doing with the car? Selling it, or keeping it and letting PC [Dorothy's husband] drive it?" He was also extremely worried about whether his mother and younger sister had enough money to live on, and he repeatedly looked into allotment checks with army officials and exhorted his mother to use the money in his private bank account in Urbana. On August 15, 1945, he writes, "As for that account of mine—I want you and Judy to have enough for everything you need. If necessary, don't hesitate to use it. You know, you say the money is mine—*but* don't forget, all the money I have or ever will have is not enough to repay you for the love and goodness given me freely by you and Dad. I'd like to pay my part on the house, too, if you would let me."

These exhortations regarding financial issues continued throughout the months, as he reassured his mother that he would continue to help with daily financial needs. On November 6, 1945, apparently responding to a comment in one of her letters, he chides, "What do you mean by that old 'pay my own way' line you are trying to feed yourself? You should know that you don't have to worry any about that. You sure supported us kids for a long enough time, so I reckon if anything happens, we sure can help you."

Another major practical issue that Dad raised often in his letters was the possibility of a bereavement discharge that would get him home ahead of the time dictated by the point system. He asked his mother to pull together paperwork, reported on what he had learned about the possibility of leaving Europe early, and weighed the advantages and disadvantages of various courses of action. By the end of August, however, he had decided that it made better sense to stay in Europe. He explains his decision to his mother in a letter dated August 31:

> *Received the affidavits, etc., today, and also another later letter. First of all, guess I'd better tell you about the papers. I talked the situation over with Major Wilcox, and McCroskery, and at present deem it advisable to just hang on to the papers and not take any action till I see how the point system is going to work out. If I took a discharge on those papers, it would not be possible to go back to school right away, and as that is what you folks want me to do—and I would like to do myself, of course—I'm not going to try for the dependency discharge right away. I believe that with a little luck I should be back in the States on points by next spring, and then I could start back to school in the fall.*

In the later months of 1945, my father repeatedly addressed the issue of his mother's employment. Oscar's death had left my grandmother with many debts and the continuing responsibility for a fourteen-year-old daughter. Not surprisingly, she found it necessary to go to work, but my father was clearly unhappy with her doing so. His tone varied in his letters—sometimes it was discouraging, sometimes jocular, sometimes patronizing—but clearly he had taken his role as man of the family to heart and felt it appropriate to pass judgment on his mother's employment activities. His first line of attack was to convince her not to find employment (July 21, 1945: "I reiterate my statement in previous letters [How you like those 10 buck words?] you do not go to work, Mom. Doggone it, do you think I want my Mom working?"). He was discouraged when she did not take this advice (August 31, 1945: "So you are going to work? I don't like that, but inasmuch as I am here and you are in Urbana, there isn't much I can do about it"), but then he found something somewhat more encouraging to say (September 7, 1945: "So you're a sales clerk now, Mom. Just turn on that old personality of yours, and I'm sure you're bound to charm the most particular customer into buying your goods. By the way, what do you sell?"). However, he was never fully happy that his mother was part of the work force, especially if it meant taking on what he viewed as menial employment (October 3, 1945: "Listen, Mom, if you can't get a decent job, don't take one at all. Let's have no more of this 'dishwasher' nonsense. I don't see any reason why you can't be one of the 'estimated ten million unemployed in the United States'").

The letters during this period also reflect a change in my father's relationship with his younger sister. Throughout his time in the army, Dad had written letters to Judy, asked about her in the general family letters, and clearly taken pride in his "big brother" role. For example, in a letter sent April 9, 1944, from Camp Blanding, he had told this story:

> *Oh yes, Judy—this is for you. After rifle inspection yesterday, Lt. Levy inspected the huts. He walked by my shelf, stopped, looked at your picture, then called me over.*
>
> *Lt. Levy—"This your sister, Miller?"*
>
> *Me—"Yes sir. She's 12 years old."*
>
> *Lt. Levy (to Sgt. Putnam)—"I had that wolfish gleam in my eye. So he tells me how old she is."*

After my grandfather's death, however, there was a subtle shift in the tone of my father's long-distance relationship with his sister. He asked frequently about her grades (November 1, 1945: "So Judy is getting all A's? Well, nice going"), commented on her boyfriends (same letter: "And going out with Tom Stephens? I don't know him, but if he is anything like Lew, Jr. he is a swell kid"), and told her about his experiences with teachers at the high school. In many of the comments, his tone moved beyond the curiosity and support of a brother and became more paternal. He frequently emphasized his expectation that she perform well in school. On September 18 he tells his mother, "So I still got a rep at Urbana High, eh? I'm sure Judy will do better than I did there." In a letter dated September 27, 1945, he encourages Judy in her schoolwork (and shows off a bit): "Mom tells me you are studying about King Tutankahmen (only she said Tut) of Egypt, Judy. If I were home I might give you a little help, but I sure wouldn't write it for you. The only way you can learn anything is by doing it." And his high expectations for his sister went beyond the classroom. In a letter to Judy on October 19, 1945, after she had joined the school yearbook staff, he instructs her on the importance of excellence in all activities: "And you are on the Rosemary now, and in SK [Sigma Kappa] and GAA [Girls Athletic Association]. You are certainly going in for a lot of extra-curricular activity. Get as much out of it as you can, because the more things you do in high school, the more fun you have. Boy, by the time you get to be a senior, you will really be something—editor of the Rosemary, president of SK and GAA, and chief drum majorette."

Thus, in many ways, my father began to take on the role of paterfamilias, and he reported that he was even taking on some of his father's idiosyncrasies. On October 15, 1945, he writes, "You know, I think I am getting some of Dad's habits. Like coffee and doughnuts late at night. . . . And the way I laugh reminds me of Dad, when I laugh unconsciously. And I still stick my tongue out a little when working on something." But he was not just a man in the family; he was also a man in the world, and my father's letters during this period communicated to his mother that he had matured in many ways, and that he understood the world beyond rural Illinois. For example, after exchanging letters with his older sister about a racy novel of the time, he writes to his mother on August 31, 1945, "So you think *Forever Amber* is trash, Mom? But you'd like to read it, though, wouldn't you, Mom? Haven't you heard, your son is a big boy, now, who does not blush easily due to a year and a half of army life." And, on September 27, he explains to his mother why the Army employs many civilian Englishwomen in post-war Europe: "These English girls get officers' privileges for doing enlisted man's work. And that is what they were hired for, as anyone with any sense can figure out. To provide entertainment for the brass, if you know what I mean."

Thus, my father's correspondence with his mother during his final months in Europe shows that he had matured in several ways. As a man, he now understood the sometimes unseemly ways of the world. As a man, he was able to take on the role of advisor and protector of his family and to make financial decisions for them; he was willing and able—was, indeed, obliged—to take on responsibility for his mother and his younger sister.

From Boy to Man—A Family Transition

The transition from childhood and adolescence to adulthood can be marked in many ways. Some of these are natural processes in the life history of an individual and a family—going away to college, getting a full-time job, marrying, having children. At other times, a rupture in family life creates the catalyst for such a transition—death or serious illness, for instance, or financial crisis. Further, these family transitions take place within a cultural, political, and economic context. Growing up is a very different experience for individuals of different socioeconomic strata, of different cultural and ethnic backgrounds, and at different historical periods. Consider the contrast in the transition between childhood and adulthood for a child in the sweatshop culture of the industrial revolution, a child in the American suburbs during the baby boom, and a child today in war-torn twenty-first-century Afghanistan. Clearly, the events in our lives are tempered by circumstance.

For my father, the transition from boyhood to manhood was conditioned by both history and family events. Historically, he was a child of the Great Depression, and this clearly influenced his ideas of what it meant to be a man. His earliest memories were of his father looking for work, struggling to keep food on the table. Financial struggles continued even after my grandfather achieved his dream of owning a print shop; when he died, he left his wife with numerous debts. The historical fact of World War II also impinged on my father's transition from boyhood to manhood. He had only one semester of college before the army claimed him. And on a personal level, the possibility of a "natural" transition to adulthood for Dad was negated by the sudden death of his father. As the only son, my father had to take on the trappings of manhood quickly.

Research on the process of growing up provides several alternatives for constructions of manhood that could be adopted given these events. For example, scholarship considering the effects of the Great Depression on the transition from youth to adulthood suggests that because men had been "demoralized" by economic hardship in the 1930s, the transition to manhood came to be defined largely through the ability to work, especially in manual labor.[7] Jeffrey Ryan Suzik argues this point in his analysis of the Civilian Conservation Corps during the 1930s: "Bigger bodies might make men feel more manly; but work, quite simply, made one a man."[8]

The events of World War II also offer alternative constructions of manhood for those growing up in that era. For men left working on the home front, a version of "rough manhood" developed in the aggressive subculture of manufacturing and industry.[9] Christina Jarvis argues that the vision of American masculinity during World War II was shaped by images of the soldier's youthful, muscular, and typically white body. She argues that this embodied construction contributed to "the creation and maintenance of a hegemonic militarized masculinity that emerged in and across U.S. institutions."[10] Susan Faludi, in her book *Stiffed,* provides a somewhat different account, maintaining that the most prevalent construction of manhood during World War II was the one propagated by Ernie Pyle in his writings from the front lines of the war. His columns from Europe downplayed the glamorous "flyboy" in favor of the beleaguered private in the foxhole. As Faludi writes, "the foot soldier was elevated into a masculine emblem—a man who proved his virility not by individual feats of showy heroism but by being quietly *useful* in conducting a war and supporting the welfare of his unit."[11]

The literature on father-son relationships also provides insights into my father's transition from boy to man. His relationship with his father was very close and affectionate, perhaps typical of father-son relationships in the early part of the twentieth century, a period that Margaret Marsh has labeled one of "masculine domesticity."[12] This close relationship—and the amount of time my father spent with his father hunting, fishing, and following their favorite sports teams—predicted positive results for my father's development. As Mark Morman and Kory Floyd conclude after a review of the literature, the "research indicates that men who are actively involved in raising their sons can have an overwhelmingly positive impact on the life course their sons pursue."[13] The extent to which Dad felt such a positive impact is evident in his birthday letter to Oscar, in which he insisted that if he could only do as well in his life as Oscar had done, he would consider himself truly successful. Dan Kindlon and Michael Thompson have found that most men want to make a better job of parenting than their fathers did.[14] But I believe my father would have thought it superfluous to try to outdo Oscar at that.

Finally, scholarship on parental death offers an additional view of the transition into adulthood. Suni Petersen and Silvia Rafuls write about the death of a parent as a time when the child "receives the scepter" and assumes a leadership role in the larger family system. In discussing the mindset of participants in their research who had lost a parent in early adulthood, they write that "fulfilling their obligations was extremely important to most of [them]."[15] In addition to discussing the concept of "receiving the scepter" and taking on the responsibilities of family life, Debra Umberson also discusses parental death as a time of reflection and re-evaluation in which the child must create a new identity as a fatherless, motherless, or orphaned adult.[16]

For my father, a confluence of several of these factors defined the transition from boyhood to manhood. Given his childhood experiences in the Great Depression and his close relationship with his father, the notion of taking care of family was an important facet of his developing definition of what it meant to be a man. He saw families as those who take care of each other—in all economic times—and he wanted to take care of his mother and his younger sister. In terms of war experience, my father largely rejected the hyper-masculine version of manhood proposed by either the "rough manhood" of the factory or the glamorous vision of the flyboy, and instead embraced the hardworking vision of Ernie Pyle—though in a less idealized form than the classic "GI Joe" persona. And although Dad in some ways embraced the notion of "taking on the scepter" of family leadership after his father's death, he clearly did not have the time (or perhaps maturity) to engage in much reflection on the meaning of his new adult role. But these ideas of caretaking, hard work, and duty to family coalesced for him into what I believe defined his idea of family manhood throughout his life—the concept of *responsibility.*

As my father entered into manhood during and after the war, as he and my mother raised their family of four daughters, and as those daughters were launched into their adult lives, my father clearly defined manhood as an acceptance of responsibility for self and family. For Dad this responsibility was multi-faceted. It meant behaving in a moral and ethical way. It meant taking care of others. It meant owning up to obligations. And it meant encouraging others to do the same. These various meanings of responsibility permeated the rest of his life through his decisions about child-rearing, friendship, family finances (which he tracked tirelessly in a pocket notebook during early retirement), and politics. In fact his attitude toward responsibility even determined his attitude toward his daughters' husbands. I recall the great pride my father showed in talking about his four eventual sons-in-law (after two of us had first husbands whom he clearly did not like). Dad's pride in these men was not in their wealth, prospects, or even their accomplishments, but rather in their sense of responsibility to their wives, themselves, and their children. These were men he was proud to have as part of his family.

Of course, my father's beliefs about family relationships and manhood were not immune to change. Though he felt that it was his responsibility to take care of his mother and he therefore resisted her desire to work, he clearly respected the role of women in the workplace. He strongly supported my mother's career in journalism, and he encouraged his daughters to aspire toward careers. Thus, in his middle years and at the end of his life, he held his view of responsible manhood in conjunction with a view of independent (and responsible) womanhood. But throughout his life, my father maintained the core beliefs about manhood that had developed through his Depression-era childhood, his wartime experiences, and the sudden death of his father. His belief in the importance of responsibility endured, a fact reflected in the life he lived. Recall the words from my father's birthday letter to his father: "You know, Dad if I can only be as good a man as you are someday, I'll consider myself a success in this world—because with me YOU'RE a tremendous success. I hope I've lived up to your expectations as a son. I know I'm no good as a soldier, but I hope you still consider me o.k. as a son." I think there is little doubt that if he had seen the respect for responsibility that my father had throughout his life, my grandfather would have judged him as even better than "o.k."

CHAPTER FOUR

Buddies and Girlfriends

Entering the armed forces always involves a sharp rupture of existing friendships and imposes an almost immediate necessity for establishing new relationships in a strange and distant environment and an esoteric occupational culture. . . . Friendship at once becomes a necessity for survival rather than a purely social activity.

ROGER LITTLE, *Friendships in the Military Community*

THE *1943 ROSEMARY,* Urbana High School's yearbook for my father's senior year, paints an idyllic picture of high school life in the 1940s. There are pages devoted to sports teams, student council, and cheer squads, photos of homeroom classes and honor societies, and a large spread devoted to theater productions of *The Imaginary Invalid* and *The Man Who Came to Dinner.* The outside world intrudes a little on this carefree picture, as two pages are devoted to "Urbana High in the War," and the editor's introduction notes that "we've taken our studying a bit more seriously this year, for the war had its effect on all of us. We all bought our share of saving stamps. . . . The girls folded bandages and knitted for the Red Cross. . . . The boys collected scrap metal. . . . They talked 'Air Corps' and compared draft numbers, and several left us to 'join up.'"[1] This was the reality as my father and other members of the class of 1943 graduated.

According to the *Rosemary,* 174 seniors graduated from Urbana High in 1943. My father was at the top of his class academically, one of four valedictorians. The face that looks out from his senior picture is serious (he is one of only two boys wearing glasses) and more youthful than the faces of many members of his class. The yearbook lists his full name—"Joe Ted Miller"—but no nickname, although nicknames ("Mac," "Junie," "Doc") accompany many of the other entries. His listed activities are academic societies, the State Latin Contest, and work as sports editor on the school paper. Thirty-three of Dad's classmates signed his yearbook, most with simple signatures, but a few with additional notes wishing him good luck or referring to his academic prowess with monikers such as "Prof" and "Brains." Some of the signatures came from girls in the class, though none of these young ladies were romantic interests. As my father reported in his memoirs, "I never had a 'date' in high school. None. Zilch."

If not for the war, the next few years of my father's life would have unfolded in predictable fashion. He would have attended the University of Illinois, probably still living at home and continuing his close connections with relatives and family friends. Living at home would have allowed him to continue his relationships with high school classmates who were also still in town, but he would undoubtedly have made new friends at college. He would probably have kept his job as a sports writer for the *News-Gazette,* thus continuing his connections with both the hometown newspaper and local coaches and players. In essence, the social network of his youth—family, friends, community members—would have continued, and it would have been enriched with new friends through college and work. Who knows, he might have even gone out on a date.

But the war intruded. After a semester at the University of Illinois, my father was drafted, and he reported for duty. He would be moving far away from the home, family, and friends who had defined his life for many years. The knowledge that this was happening to other young men all around the country was probably only slightly comforting for this eighteen-year-old who described himself as "self-conscious around other people who were not family or close friends." The rest of this chapter, then, will review my father's experiences with friendship and (to a lesser extent) romance during the months of his military service and will look at ways in which these wartime relationships may have shaped his later social life. After considering my father's months of basic training and his efforts to make friends, his choice of buddies, and the nature of his relationships with "the boys," I will examine the ways in which these relationships both continued and evolved during his months in Europe. After a brief look at my father's connections with home-front friends and his romantic interests, I will examine the ways in which his relationships can be seen as the "rule" or the "exception" to existing theory and research on friendship. Finally, I will consider the ways in which my father's experiences with buddies and girlfriends during the war shaped the nature of his relationships in later life.

Buddies during Basic

> Mine was limited service. Perforated eardrum. It was stateside all the way, safe and uneventful. Yet I remember, in surprising detail, the uneventful events; and all those boy-faces, pimply, acned, baby-smooth, and bewildered.
>
> JAMES SANDERS, IN STUDS TERKEL'S *The Good War*

When my father arrived at Camp Blanding in Florida on February 1, 1944, he had been away from home for less than a week. During that time he had gone through the busyness of induction activities at Fort Sheridan and had traveled a thousand miles on a crowded train. In one of his first letters home, he let his folks know that he had "a terrific case of homesickness" but hoped it would pass. He knew that his best chance of feeling better was making some friends, but he worried whether that would be possible, given that the men in his barracks were all at least a decade older than he was, and married. But in the next two days, as new men came in, beginning with Red Whitmire from St. Louis, who knew Dad's old friends Jack Gordon and Tommy Hamilton, the picture brightened. In the following weeks at Camp Blanding, Dad did make friends. At first these were the younger kids in his barracks whom he saw as "like" him in some way. There was Joe Dibrell, who played chess. Tom Alagna, a printer's devil before the army. Cal Melson and Gene Hill, the "swell fellows" who bunked in his hut. On February 10, Dad happily reports, "I feel I have a very good friend—interesting, fun, clean—in Chuck Jones, a 180-pound husky from Minneapolis, Minn. We just returned from getting Pepsi at the PX & he is sitting beside me now writing to his girl." And later in his time at Blanding, my father developed friendships with other soldiers in code training.

It is not surprising that in making friends my father gravitated toward the "boys" who were most like him. He found these similarities in various ways. He befriended others who liked sports (and was quite impressed when he found out that one of his hut-mates played for a minor league Yankees team) or who were interested in reading and education or were motivated and skilled enough for advanced radio training, or who just liked Pepsi-Cola and good, clean fun.

Age was a particularly important issue among soldiers, and a division apparently developed at Camp Blanding between the younger and older recruits. On March 27 Dad writes, "Some of the older guys down here are beginning to grate on my nerves. For instance, there are 2 men over 35 in my hut—one with 7 kids. These two treat us 18-year-olds as children. They act so superior & 'bossy' just as if they knew everything—we knew nothing. So far, me & Steve & Kurt & the rest of us have kept quiet, letting them blow, but someday—."

Dad's pattern of seeking out "friends like me" continued at Camp Van Dorn in Mississippi. He was at first horribly homesick (as he had been at the start of training in Florida), evidently in part because he was uncomfortable establishing friendships with men whose interests, centered on drinking, gambling, and womanizing, contrasted with his own quiet bookishness. But at this camp, too, he soon found others with whom he could connect. At Van Dorn, he made two very good friends: Harold "Shorty" West ("a little fat kid. He's in I & R (Intelligence and Reconnaissance)—a headquarters company man, like myself"), and Ernest "Barney" Forrest ("18—One of my pals—rather plump—loves sleeping & eating. Has a good nature").

At both Blanding and Van Dorn, these friendships revolved around activities like attending movies, going to the PX, hanging out and shooting the breeze in the dayroom or the barracks, and sharing the goodies in packages from home. On two occasions, Harold West took over on a letter Dad was writing his folks in Urbana. On September 24 the letter reads, "This hand writing has changed. Well so has the one writing it. I am Harold. Joe and myself always go around together." Again, on October 18, "Joe had to go out and finish filling out some papers so he asked me to finish this. We always go around together. We are going to see 'Atlantic City' tonight. All there is to do is go to shows." There may not have been a great deal of excitement at Camp Van Dorn, but at least Joe and Harold were able to "go around together."

Time with friends became somewhat more exciting when there were opportunities to enjoy a pass in town or even go on leave together to a distant city. There were also occasional hijinks on base. On April 30 Dad reports, "We sure had a lot of fun in the hut after I wrote last night. Dave Palmer came over from next door, & he & I & Cal Melson—only ones there—performed these deeds: (1-) Short-sheeted Kreider's bed, so when he climbed in he would only slide in halfway then get caught in the sheets, (2-) Sewed up the sleeves of the fatigue shirts of Pohlmann, Leiserowitz, & Hoover, (3-) Put a broomstick in Malloy's bed, (4-) Sewed Kressley's towel around his hanger."

Throughout the development of these buddy relationships at both Camp Blanding and Camp Van Dorn, my father's letters exhibited an interesting tension regarding his desire to be "one of the boys." His desire for inclusion can be seen in his reports about card games (February 13: "using my toothpicks for money—what a gang") and sports discussions (April 7: "I hear a baseball argument in the back of the hut, & I want to join in"). Clearly, though, being one of the boys also meant not sticking out too much. For example, on February 13, he asks for his mother to send down his "Tonette" because "everyone seems to have a harmonica, ocarina, or jewsharp, & I wouldn't want to be different," and on April 23 he laments that "the boys" made fun of his loud swimming trunks and notes that he will "get a nice conservative pair before I go swimming again."

But when it came to some of the most popular activities of the soldiering life—drinking and, to a lesser extent, "womanizing"—my father expressed absolutely no desire to be part of the gang. He writes several times early in his stay at Blanding about parties that he opted out of (February 21: "I hate beer & women—so I'm not going") or that he was happy to have missed (March 5: "Our platoon's party last night was pretty liquid I guess. I'm really glad I didn't go"). In March, a series of letters demonstrated the strength of his opposition to "fitting in" with these kinds of activities.

> MARCH 16, 1944: *I've been pretty mad today—me and several others in the platoon. There's going to be a company party Saturday night—"whisky, wine, & women," in the words of the C.O. Everyone going has to chip in $1 to add to the Co. fund.* I am not going. *So, today we who decided not to go were told to either go or draw some detail over the weekend. I think it's pretty high-handed.*

> MARCH 17, 1944: *I'm pretty darn mad at this army, company, & platoon. The guys who refused to kick in a buck for their whisky & Wacs at the party tomorrow night have to stand guard outside the doors. A pretty raw deal, if you ask me. I have lost all faith in any fairness the army ever thought it possessed.*

> MARCH 19, 1944: *The guard duty at the party I told you about turned out to be a farce. I sat on the step about 10 minutes & then was told to leave or go inside any time I pleased. I went inside & Hoover—guy in my hut who is acting sergeant—was waiting on the bar. He knew I didn't like any of their drinks, so he slipped me a quart—a full quart—of straight ginger ale & I beat it back to the hut & read & ate crackers & drank ginger ale.*

Thus, throughout his months of basic training, my father developed friendships that were probably similar to those he had in high school. They were with "boys" who were a lot like him in age, background, and interests, and he hung out with these buddies on the base and, occasionally, farther afield with off-base passes. He felt disdain, however, for the penchant many of the men had for alcohol. This attitude did not seem to make him an outcast, however, as he gravitated toward others who shared his values—though perhaps they were less vociferous about them. Commenting on the disgust he felt with hungover members of his platoon on the morning following the party described above, he concludes, "I was happy to see none of my friends drinking much."

Buddies Overseas

> I remember those Hollywood films where people sat in their trenches and had ideological discussions about the beauties of democracy at home. Oh, bullshit! I remember those movies. They were stupid. You don't talk during combat. There's a strange closeness of the men.
>
> RICHARD LEACOCK, IN STUDS TERKEL'S *The Good War*

When my father shipped overseas in December of 1944, he went with the men he had served with at Camp Van Dorn—members of the 63rd Infantry Division. Sadly, one of his closest friends at Van Dorn, Harold West, was in a different regiment, so they were split up soon after they arrived in Europe. For the core of the communications platoon, however, there was a continuation of relationships formed during training. But the nature of my father's friendships changed during his time in the ETO, both in terms of the way he thought about his buddies and the activities that constituted their relationships.

Once on the battlegrounds of France and Germany before V-E Day, my father's former pattern of establishing a few close friendships with people of like age and interests fell by the wayside. Close friendships were now far less important than comradeship in the group as a whole, and my father was much less concerned with the issue of similarity. And he was also better disposed to like the men generally. On March 4, 1945, Dad describes his fellow members of the radio section, all in positive terms and without any mention of age. He notes that "all have some college education—so you see, I am associating with a fine group of fellows," and he doesn't disparage any of them as he often had during basic training. At Camp Van Dorn he had described one of the men in his barracks as "T/5 Vaughan—Radioman. Has job of driving the radio chief. I like him *least.* He's about 21, & well educated. And does he know it. He tries to boss everyone he meets. A jerk of the first water, in my opinion." A few months later, and in the midst of battle, the description of the same man has changed to "T-5 Edward 'Ned' Vaughan—a rather sophisticated New Yorker, but nevertheless very agreeable." My father also became less judgmental about the drinking, which—not surprisingly—was more prevalent in Europe. Soon after landing, on Christmas Day, he notes that his section chief opened up a celebratory bottle from the States and says, "I even took a shot of it this morning just to make the Christmas spirit uniform in the CP."

The activities that marked my father's friendships also changed once he was in Europe. This was to be expected, of course, as there was no longer a clear structure of "work time" and "off time," there were no movies to attend or service clubs to hang out in, and there were no evening passes or weekend leaves to nearby towns. Instead, the focus was largely on work and survival—and a buddy was somebody who could help you accomplish a difficult task under difficult circumstances. But there were also many times when the men created opportunities for fun in the midst of war. Sometimes this happened when the regiment was on the move and there was a chance to hunt local wildlife. At other times, openings for fun came when the soldiers finally occupied a village or town and were able to string up lines for a phonograph or to ride around on abandoned motorbikes. The times my father enjoyed most were evenings when he and his friends found food and cooked it up and when the musicians in the group provided entertainment (March 24, 1945: "We had some pretty good music with an accordion, a fiddle, two guitars, and a harmonica"). On March 25, 1945, Dad provides an account of one such party—complete with nicknames, sound effects, and commentary:

> *Now I'd like to re-enact the scene I was a part of yesterday afternoon and evening.*
>
> *"Ah!—a package for me—with cokes in it—hooray."*
>
> *Later in evening—"Put on some water & grease—we're going for food"—this from the "Big"—"Let's get some spuds"—(The Brow says)—"A lot downstairs."*
>
> *The Big returns—sound effects: "cut-cut-cut-cock-a-doodle-doo."*
>
> *A half hour later he comes in with four chickens all dressed. "The Foot," myself, Vaughan, and Larson are peeling potatoes.*
>
> *At 10:30 French fries, French fried chicken, and (for me) cokes—ah! A perfect meal.*
>
> *(Scene ends)*

Interestingly, as the war in Europe came to a close, my father's friendships started reverting to the form they had taken during basic training. In April, Dad made a new close friend, Bob Nielsen, "a mere lad of 18 years . . . a great joker, a lot of fun." This friendship continued for several months and included a joint leave to Paris in July. Then, stationed in Paris and Versailles after the war, Dad once again began making friends of the people he worked with. He was particularly close to Cy Field, a "really swell fellow" from Buffalo, with whom he went on leave in Brussels. They took in the highbrow events of Paris (November 19, 1945: "Oh yes, Cy and I are also cultured peoples—we got tickets for the opera yesterday, and will attend next Sunday. It is supposed to be one of the 'Ritzy' things to do in Paris"); enjoyed "private parties" of cheese, nuts, olives, and champagne in their billet; and shared opinions on grooming (November 16, 1945: "For the past week I have been combing my blond locks straight back with no part in them. Cy says my hair looks better that way and I am inclined to agree with him"). The pair also discussed ways to continue their friendship when they returned home; they planned the long road trip through America and Canada discussed in chapter 2.

Friends (and Romance?) on the Home Front

Throughout his time in the army, both during stateside training and in Europe, my father worked to keep up with boyhood friends from Illinois. In his letters he often asked for updated army addresses for his friends and commented on his correspondence with them (on April 3, 1945: "I got a letter from Jack Gordon today, too. He says he is almost completely recovered now & is expecting to get a furlough to London in a short time. He says he received a letter from you recently in addition to one from me"). Dad also kept up with the changing relationships of friends at home. On December 15, 1944, he comments, "I'm dropping Betty Shinker a line tonight—first chance I've had to congratulate her. Boy was I surprised to receive that clipping about her engagement. And I thought she was going to be a career girl." And, in contrast, on November 29, 1945, he writes, "So Willa Mae Patterson and Earl Medaris are getting married? Well, it doesn't particularly surprise me. Willa Mae is a nice looking girl, and it always seemed to me that people in small rural towns invariably get married when they are young." The sad part of keeping up with friends and classmates from Illinois was when he learned of their having been injured or killed in the war. Throughout the second half of 1945, Dad's letters are scattered with comments such as "Read in one of the Gazettes where Dick Pittman of the Marines got killed on Iwo. Too bad—he was really a nice kid" (June 1) and "Too bad about Bill Latimer. He was a swell kid. But a bullet makes no distinction between people" (December 19).

Finally, it is important to consider briefly whether romantic relationships were at all part of my father's thinking during this period of his life. As noted earlier, his later-life memoir reports "zilch" dates during high school, and although an early letter from Camp Blanding about valentines hints at thoughts of romance (February 10, 1944: "Debated quite a while about sending one to J. G. but finally did it—a nice conservative one—hope she doesn't think me rude for it"), there is never another mention of "J. G." in subsequent letters. That spring, though, my father began corresponding with Caroline, a family friend whose parents ran a local business close to my grandfather's print shop.[2] Caroline was several years older than my father and attended the University of Illinois. The first mention of correspondence with her came near the end of my Dad's stay at Camp Blanding, when he wrote home on April 26, 1944, "Got letter from Caroline today. Will write her this weekend. Tell her that cartoon is definitely *not* the army."

The correspondence with Caroline continued while my father was at Camp Van Dorn (August 14: "Got an interesting letter from Caroline today. Will have to answer her in the near future—maybe tonight"; September 10: "Say, tell Caroline she still owes me a letter. Tell her I won't write her till she answers my last epistle") and picked up even more when he was overseas. Once there he sent Caroline lists of where he had been, commented on her success in school (June 20: "Boy it sure looks like Caroline is doing alright for herself. She'll probably get a darn good job out of her record alone") and received comfort from her after his father's death (July 14: "I'm enclosing a letter I got from Caroline a few days ago. I think it is one of the most beautiful letters I have ever received"). Eventually, Dad started thinking about Caroline in a different light. On July 16, 1945, he writes his mother, "You know, after prolonged correspondence, I have suddenly come to the startling realization that my friendship with Caroline is a little more than that. You might even call her my girl friend. It's a little surprising to me—I hope you don't object, Mom." Beyond this relationship with Caroline, however, my father made no mention of dating or interest in girls, save one comment in a letter of August 19, 1945, that seems more a longing for home (or hamburgers) than for romance: "Been thinking about getting a date with some WAC ever since I heard that the WACs have a hamburger and milk shake joint over on the Champs. For WACs and enlisted dates only. Boy, a good hamburger and chocolate malted would really be a taste of America again."

Friendships in Context

Peter Nardi argues that friendships between men were long seen as the model of true intimacy, and that women were often regarded as incapable of sustaining true friendship.[3] Men's friendships were nurtured in the give-and-take of public life, and close male bonding characterized by heroism, comradeship, and virtue were central to civilizations from ancient Greece through medieval Europe. This pattern continued into the nineteenth century. Daniel Webster called his best male friend "the partner of my joys, griefs, and affections, the only participator of my most secret thoughts."[4] However, in the late nineteenth and early twentieth centuries, the typical nature of male friendship shifted. The changes are usually attributed to concerns about homosexuality and to increased competition among men and the modern pressure for men to uphold norms of rationality and leave emotion to women.[5] Today, then, there are a number of "truisms" about friendship in general—and male friendship in particular—that are based on both social research and personal and cultural understandings about what it "means" to be a friend. In this section, I consider my father's relationships before and during the war in the light of these truisms, drawing conclusions about whether his experiences can be seen as the rule or the exception to these various beliefs about friendship.

SOURCES OF FRIENDSHIP—"PEOPLE LIKE ME"

Aristotle observed centuries ago that "those, then, are friends to whom the same things are good and evil; and those who are, moreover, friendly or unfriendly to the same people."[6] In other words, we tend to like and form relationships with others who have similar attitudes and tastes. This tendency to be friends with those who are like us has been called the "rule of homogamy" and has been found to hold across a variety of characteristics including education, religion, family background, social status, physical attractiveness, and interests.[7] Scott Feld and William Carter point out that we often learn about these similarities through participation in shared activities such as church, sports, and work, and that age is a particularly important demographic similarity on which individuals base their friendships.[8] As Bradford Brown argues, "Age similarity connotes common membership in a given generation or 'cohort.' Members of the same cohort not only occupy the same life stage but also share a common history. . . . Since people prefer to have friends who are similar to themselves, these commonalities clearly facilitate friendship."[9]

With regard to this central truism of friendship, my father was definitely the "rule" and not the "exception." When he arrived at each new phase of his military life, he looked around the barracks, the dayroom, the chow line, and the classroom for others who he believed shared important characteristics with him. He looked for boys recently graduated from high school who shared his respect for education, who were interested in sports, who liked to read and to play chess, and who were just "swell" kids. His letters home describing his "hut-mates" show that he liked those who had these characteristics and was critical of those who did not. Compare, for example, the thumbnail sketches of several "boys in my hut" from April 9, 1944:

- *Marvin Pohlmann—hut leader. 33. St. Louis. Worked in TNT plant. Married, 12-year-old girl. Likes his liquor on weekends.*
- *Calvin Melson—18—Lincoln, Neb. Attending U. of Neb. when draft called. Good kid with sharp wit. Athletically inclined.*
- *Tom Malloy—18. Brooklyn. One of the best. Likes to read, write. We get into some hot baseball arguments. A real pal.*
- *Gus Garvas—New York. Playboy. Always has money. Likes liquor.*

But, as I have pointed out, personal similarities became less important for my father during times of battle. Then "similarity" ceased to be about age, education, or a penchant for baseball and chess. Instead, what mattered was the shared context: the cold weather, the incoming shells, the march to the next village, the K-rations, the enemy across the river. Who cares if a guy is a playboy, uneducated, or inclined to liquor when you are counting on him to lay radio lines in the dead of night or to share a foxhole with you as you listen to nearby bombing? Indeed, "a comrade in war is a man you can trust with anything because you trust him with your life,"[10] and my father appeared to get along with pretty much everybody in his unit. However, having "friends like me" again became important to my father after the days of battle were over, and this is a pattern found in research on military friendship. Roger Little reports that the close relationships of combat buddies rarely survive long: "Even when buddies were in the reserve bivouac rather than 'on the line' in direct contact with the enemy, they became more contentious and less mutually supportive."[11]

SOURCES OF FRIENDSHIP—THE WORKPLACE

One of the most important contexts for discovering the similarities that may lead to friendship is the workplace, especially for men. A study of men living in the Detroit area in the mid-1960s found that most friendships were made at work (26 percent, compared with 23 percent for neighborhood friends and 20 percent for childhood friends).[12] More recently, an interview study of almost four hundred men in 2002 asked the question "How do you establish and maintain friendships with men?" Sixty percent of respondents noted that they looked for commonalities, and a third of respondents said that they made friends through work.[13] The importance of the workplace for forming friendship has undoubtedly grown since the industrial revolution as people moved from communal village or farm settings to more impersonal cities and then suburbs, and as work became a more central focus of many lives. As Letty Cottin Pogrebin argues, "The workplace has become the extended family, village well, and small town, all rolled into one. For many people, socializing at work is the most effortless socializing of their complex lives."[14] There are a number of reasons why the workplace serves as a crucial wellspring for friendship. The first one is simple proximity. In addition, it is likely that co-workers are similar in education and social class and that they have intersecting interests. And, as Gary Fine has found, jobs that require (or at least allow) task coordination and collaboration are especially conducive to friendship.[15] This is true because "to the extent that the work environment fosters interaction, noncompetitiveness, and interdependence between people, friendships will be more likely to form."[16]

In this friendship pattern as well, my father's experience proves the rule rather than the exception. During his basic training at Camp Blanding, many of Dad's buddies were those he had code class with—he saw them more frequently than he saw other people, they shared the challenges of increasing their "words per minute," and they were often of a similar age and level of education. At Camp Van Dorn, too, he drew many of his friends from the communications platoon, and he remained friends with them in Europe while he worked in the radio division or message center. There was more to the development of these friendships, though, than simple proximity; something in the nature of the work apparently lent itself to social activity. Indeed, at one point while at Camp Van Dorn my father was transferred to another section, and he was not happy about it. On September 30, 1944, he writes, "I don't care to work in Personnel—it's too dull & boring. True—I get a little typing practice in, but you don't have the fun you have when you're with the boys in communications. I guess I was meant to associate with & enjoy the company of other *people*—not uninteresting files. Maybe that's the reason I want to return to the newspaper game—it's so full of life & vitality." The overlap between friendship and the workplace continued in Paris and Versailles after the war. On September 3, 1945, Dad talks about weekends with the gang: "I don't know why, but all the guys who work around here invariably end up at the office sometime every Sunday or day off. We practically make it a base of operations, inasmuch as it is right in the heart of town, and has typewriters so convenient for letter writing. Right at present, just before evening chow on this Labor Day, 1945, Rasmussen is messing around with some modeling clay, Mac is writing a letter on another typewriter, Peel is reading, and Lt. Dunham is looking through the files."

MEN'S FRIENDSHIPS—"SIDE BY SIDE"

A final truism about friendships, particularly in the twentieth century, is that women's friendships are expressive and based on shared conversation and intimacy, while men's are instrumental and based in shared activities. This difference between the "face-to-face" relationships of women and the "side-by-side" relationships of men has been noted repeatedly in research; Lillian Rubin summarizes it in her remark that that men "tend to *do* rather than *be* together."[17] In a study of college friendships, men were twice as likely as women to say they preferred "doing some activity" with a best friend and sought friends who liked similar activities, while women looked for friends who felt the same way about things and chose "just talking" as the most important aspect of their friendships.[18]

In this pattern, too, my father's relationships during his adolescence and young adulthood largely followed the norm. His comments on his friends in his correspondence almost always occur in the context of activities—movies, passes into town, cooking, music at night, or just "going around" together. When there are reports about talking, the conversation is most often described as a "bull session"—usually about sports, though occasionally about superior officers or world events. There is little talk reported about feelings. Thus, my father followed the pattern of activity-based friendships that is typical for men. However, he was also a bit different from many men in that having one or two very close friends was clearly important to him. He identified particular men at various points in his time in the military—Barney Forrest, Harold West, Cy Field, Bob Nielsen—who were clearly friends across various activities and contexts and were people with whom he felt very comfortable. Victor Seidler argues that "the thinness of men's relationships with each other and ways that they seem to be constantly undermined through competition and jealousy are distinctive features of modern society."[19] However, my father's close friendships were clearly not "thin," and there was no hint about them of competitive masculinity. Instead, because my father gravitated toward those like himself, he was extremely comfortable in these relationships, even if they were not marked by the sharing of deep intimacies.

After the Army

I never joined a veterans' organization. They rub me the wrong way. These guys want to perpetuate something that should have been finished.

JOE HANLEY, IN STUDS TERKEL'S *The Good War*

In my father's small diary and datebook from his time in the ETO, one of the final pages contains the heading "Buddies' Homes" with a list of almost twenty names often mentioned in his letters—West, Bigger, Disbrow, Vaughan, Nielsen, Forrest, and others. Each name was associated with a U.S. city and state—Beloit, Wisconsin; Pittsburgh, Pennsylvania; Norfolk, Virginia; Gulfport, Mississippi. Whether this list grew from a plan to keep up with buddies after the war or was merely an accounting of friendships is not clear. But the names and hometowns were important enough to my father at the time to write down. Another section of the diary provides an accounting of my fathers' travels through an assortment of countries, states, cities, and national parks. From these lists it is clear that when my father returned from Europe, he embarked on a trip that took him from Illinois through the western part of the United States and into Canada, visiting such national parks as Badlands, Black Hills, Rushmore, Yellowstone, Glacier, and Banff. I assume this was the road trip that he and Cy Field planned during their last few months in post-war France. However, I never heard anything about it growing up, and my mother only vaguely recalled hearing my father talk about it—and she thought the trip was with high school friend John Parry, not a war buddy.

Research literature and popular writing alike reflect a divergence of opinion about whether wartime friendships endure. Stephen Ambrose writes about the friendships formed by members of the Easy Company, 506th Parachute Infantry Regiment, 101st Airborne, after talking with them many years after their enlistment:

> *As they talked about other members of the company, about various reunions over the decades it became obvious that they continued to be a band of brothers. Although they were scattered all across the North American continent and overseas, they knew each other's wives, children, grandchildren, each other's problems and successes. They visited regularly, kept in close contact by mail and by phone. They helped each other in emergencies and times of trouble. And the only thing they had in common was their three-year experiences in World War II, when they had been thrown together by the U.S. Army.*[20]

But other commentators argue that relationships forged in war are unlikely to continue. Lillian Rubin says, "Margaret Mead, writing after our last heroic war, World War II, noted that English observers watching American buddy relationships were confused by the fact that our soldiers seemed to suffer intense grief at the death of a buddy yet, on close examination, the relationships were found to be extremely transitory."[21] Rubin goes on to note about her own research that "among the men I met, not one veteran of the wars in Vietnam and Korea retained anything more than a superficial relationship with the buddies who were so important to them then. They sang 'Auld Lang Syne' together when they met, stirring fond memories and reawakening the emotional bond for a moment. But there was no intimacy between them."[22] In *The Warriors,* J. Glenn Gray makes a similar point in distinguishing between true friends and "comrades": "Comrades love one another like brothers, and under the influence of shared experience commonly vow to remain true friends for the rest of their lives. But when other experiences intervene and common memories dim, they gradually become strangers."[23]

My father was definitely on the second end of this continuum. Beyond the (presumed) trip with Cy Field during the summer of 1946, he maintained no contact with his war buddies. He never attended a reunion and was not a member of veterans' groups such as the VFW or the American Legion. There were never any get-togethers or phone calls later in life, and—as far as anyone in our family can remember—there was never a war buddy on my parents' extensive Christmas card list. This is not to suggest that all memory of the war was excised from my dad's life—he obviously kept the correspondence his mother had saved, as well as his field jacket, his medals and citations, his diary, and a box of assorted memorabilia. And though he was not given to telling war stories, he was eager to talk with me about his experiences when we toured the ETO displays at the Eisenhower Presidential Museum in Abilene, Kansas. But these memories were never connected to individual buddies, and there was no continuation of the relationships that had been very important to him for several years of his life.

So what *did* happen in my father's relationships when he returned from the war? He reconnected with old friends from high school and family, and a few of these Urbana connections—John Parry and others—remained on the Christmas card list for many years to come and even warranted occasional phone calls and visits. The question of what happened with Caroline upon my father's return to the States is not clear, however. While I was transcribing my father's letters, my curiosity was piqued by the ongoing and frequent references to Caroline. I was able to find family contact information on the Internet, and I sent an e-mail asking about the relationship. Caroline's daughter responded that my father and Caroline were just wartime correspondents and that there was no romance involved. I later found some journaling my dad did while recovering from a stroke in which he reports that they did date after the war but that it never got beyond "heavy smooching."

The exact nature of this relationship may never be known. However, what is most interesting about Caroline is not the mystery but the standard she set for future relationships. Caroline was undoubtedly a very smart young woman—she was well-educated, a lively correspondent, and successful in her career. As my mother recently commented when I talked with her about Caroline, "Yes, that's exactly the kind of girl your dad would want as a girlfriend." My father lived in Urbana for several years after he returned from the war and then moved to San Antonio, New Orleans, and Detroit. There was no serious girlfriend in either post-war Urbana or during his brief stay in San Antonio. But he was smitten by a young woman he worked with at the *New Orleans Item.* Apparently, he thought she might be "the one," but she instead married a close mutual friend and moved on to a career at the *Washington Post.*

So my father's luck in romance had not been particularly good when he moved back to the Midwest to take a job at the *Detroit Free Press.* Ever the sports lover, he took advantage of some free tickets to a Detroit Tigers game in the early fall of 1952. My mother was at that game with Jim Wilson—someone she had been "going around with" and one of my father's co-workers at the *Free Press.* When Jim saw my father, he suggested to Mom that they go talk with "the new guy," and the rest is family lore. My father had theater tickets a few weeks later and he called this "Margaret Hyde" girl to see if she wanted to go. Legend has it that she didn't answer the call, so he went alone. She did answer the phone a week later, and they attended a Red Wings hockey game for a first date. Then, in a few days, he called her after work reporting that he was "at loose ends," and she surprised him by inviting him over to her apartment. My mother recently told me that it was a "successful date." Within weeks, it was clear where the relationship was going, and Joe and Margaret were married at the end of March, 1953. I recently asked my mother if Dad had ever proposed. "Well, sort of . . . he said 'you know what I want—I don't want anything temporary.'" A proposal of sorts, and she was quite happy with it. My mother was thirty years old at the time, and my father was twenty-eight. They both wanted marriage and children. My mother told me, "This was a nice guy who wanted to marry me and who I could marry. It wasn't really passion, but it was a good friendship, and it worked."

In the following decades, my father continued to follow the friendship patterns that he had established in his youth. He drew his few close friends from among his work colleagues. He was happiest socializing with other journalists at the *Free Press* and their spouses, and his friendships with them were the most enduring of his adult life. His friendships continued to be based principally on shared activities (work, tennis, bridge) rather than on intimate conversation. In middle life, my parents' friendships continued to fall in line with the truisms of the literature on friendship. One of these is that many men find their strongest emotional support, companionship, and intimacy in marriage rather than friendship.[24] This was indisputably true of my father. My mother was clearly his major source of intimacy and support throughout their fifty-three-year marriage.

Another truism from the research is that wives are often the driving force behind couples' social lives. "Often, the men like each other and their wives, but that is not necessary. As long as the wives like each other, mere toleration on the part of the men is all that is necessary."[25] This pattern was not quite so true of my parents, as two of their most important "couple" friends involved men from the newspaper. And my father did little to become part of my mother's network of friends.

Thus, there was a consistent pattern to my father's friendships throughout his life, and it comported with a lot of what we know about men's friendships. What is sad, however, is the equally predictable course of his friendships in later life. Research suggests that as men age, they tend to have fewer friendships than women because "as families are formed, the wife and children increasingly pull men away from friends."[26] Then there is retirement, and the workplace is no longer available to form and reinforce friendships based on shared activities and interests. The isolating influence of retirement was exacerbated for my parents when they moved to Florida, far away from their contacts in Detroit. This was not a problem for my mother—when she arrived in Sarasota she joined a church, participated in the local AAUW chapter, taught macramé to the blind, and formed a bridge group. My father made some fledgling efforts at friendship, but his reticent personality and his lifelong penchant for "friends like me" kept him from forming any connections. Instead, he watched TV and read, swam in the pool, worked on some writing, planned trips, and served as a "house-husband." As my sister Mary remembered, "once he was retired, his circle got smaller and smaller. Mother, of course, was everything to him—he had his family, and he didn't seem to need much more socially. Which meant he grew more and more isolated."

It is hard to determine the degree to which my father's later-life friendships were presaged by his experiences in World War II. His friendships during the war followed a pattern dictated by his gender, personality, and childhood experiences—a few close relationships with "boys" like him and comfortable relationships with comrades-in-arms. But when he returned from the war, these relationships fell by the wayside, perhaps through lack of effort but probably also by choice. In those first few years, he seemed to follow the pattern of Michael Gold, one of the World War II veterans described by Thomas Childers in *Soldier from the War Returning*: "He was not interested in the war, he told himself. He didn't talk about it with other veterans at Cornell or at work during the summer. It was over, irrelevant to the life he wanted to lead now."[27] Later in life, too, my father could be described using the same words Childers used to describe Michael Gold: "People liked him; he was brilliant and funny. But he was not easy to know. He had no real friends, no one to confide in. . . . He was most comfortable, he came to realize, in the company of women."[28]

Though there is a public image of veterans sharing both memories and plans in American Legion Halls, Michael Gold and my father may well be more typical. There is a bit of sadness to their pattern that can result in late-life isolation. But when I look at my father's life, I also see another side to the coin: I see the joy apparent in a picture of him with his friends from the newsroom as they threw him a bachelor's party. I recall the joy of the times during my childhood when I sat on the stairs above the living room, listening to my parents' small group of friends in lively conversation over brandy, and the joy of family times when all that mattered was Mom and Dad and the four Miller girls. Yes, the patterns of my father's friendships were predictable, and predictably led to some loneliness. But these patterns also led to clear joy among family—and a few close friends. And for that, I am grateful.

CHAPTER FIVE

Work and Bureaucracy

> Years later, people who had grown up during the worst times of The Great Depression looked back with a certain pride. . . . Hard times had propelled them into the adult world much sooner than they might have wished, yet they had discovered within themselves strengths and skills that would last throughout their lives.
>
> RUSSELL FREEDMAN, *Children of the Great Depression*

CHILDREN AND ADOLESCENTS TODAY learn about work in many different places and ways: at home, at school, from part-time employment, and from television, movies, and the internet.[1] But my father, growing up during the Great Depression, did not have this ubiquity of avenues for learning about work and the workplace. Dad's father had difficulty finding work as a printer during much of the 1930s, though by the time Dad left for basic training, Oscar Miller had opened his own print shop. Dad obviously knew something about the operation of the shop (setting the type, running the press, embossing), but it is not clear that he had much understanding or respect for the print shop as a business. He repeatedly sent his father requests for stationery for his buddies, and in a letter dated March 12, 1944, along with an order for a friend, he included some ribbing about his father's shop as a profitable enterprise: "By the way, Joe wants a little stationery, too. Put on it JOSEPH B. DIBRELL & U.S. Army. Same as mine. Now listen to this. Joe absolutely & positively refused to take it unless he paid me. Now you do this, & send me the bill, no *DO IT!!!!!!* Heck, you've got to make a little money in the printing business."

There was also some limited learning about work in the Miller household. While growing up, my father undoubtedly had assigned chores, though his younger sister remembered him as being more or less exempt from housework. It was typical of the era for work to be largely segregated along gender lines, and that my father benefited from such a division of labor can be deduced from the following letter to his mother, dated April 16, 1944:

I also wanted to tell you of some of my household accomplishments to date:

1. *I have learned to make a bed very efficiently, neatly, & tightly. Average time—3 to 5 minutes. Of course that's a single bed.*
2. *Wash clothes (prior to receiving your fine shipment of clothes.)*
3. *Cook. It may be just heating C rations in cans, but it's still cooking.*
4. *Sweep, mop, & scrub. Sweep & mop every day, scrubbing every Fri. nite*
5. *Wash dishes, etc., Peel potatoes. Results of K.P.*
6. *Shine shoes—achieving a bright polish.*
7. *Sew. Not good, but buttons, tears, & small patches.*

Don't you think I'd make some fine woman a good wife? (End of joke, laff here—ha ha ha)

In his job as a stringer reporting on high school and junior high sporting events for the local newspaper, my father also had some teenage experience with paid employment.

It was, however, sporadic and independent—he probably had deadlines to meet, but he did not punch a time clock. Thus, his experiences with the workplace were somewhat limited when he entered the army, but they ramped up quickly in the early months of basic training. In addition to undergoing physical conditioning and weapons training, Dad was experiencing a crash course in the world of work. Part of this introduction meant developing a clearer understanding of his own competencies in completing various assignments. Part involved improving his knowledge of the ins and outs of hierarchy and bureaucracy. And part involved learning about occupational differences and divisions. Many of these strands of understanding are represented in a letter he sent home on May 10, 1944, describing a particularly successful day of work:

Dear Folks,

Riding the gravy train today, thanks to Lt. Levy. A summary of events since my last letter.

Last night, as we were marching out of the area with full fields en route to classes till 10:30, Lt. Levy called me out, told me to get rid of my pack & report to the orderly room. So for about ½ hour I stuff envelopes. Then,

Lt. Levy—"can you type, Miller? Corp. Corcoran isn't doing so well."

Me—"Yes sir."

Lt. Levy—"Go to work."

So for the next 3 hours I typed Signal Operations Instruction Sheets, Authenticators, & other name sheets. Every time I turn around Lt. Levy says, "Say, you're really fast Joe. We've really got this thing licked."

Then this morning me & the others went out to the Bivouac area. So we provide communications between h.q. & the company commanders via the SCR 536. Boy, I was stationed with a rifle company captain & he invariably advanced ahead of his troops—and I had to stick by him.

For a while I really got scared. It was just like a battle. Machine gun fire kicking up dust 10 yards ahead of you, mortar & howitzer shells hitting a little further out, & about 200 yards out heavy artillery dropping.

But I was the boss out there. The captain I was with couldn't move till I have him orders from h.q. Communications is really *the important thing.*

Then this afternoon about 1:30 Lt. Levy called me out of class—no one else, just me—& says he wants my help.

So we walk slowly from the code room back to the company area, Lt. Levy telling me his life history in a very friendly way. Back in the area, Lt. Levy says, "Joe, you've worked pretty hard last nite & today. Go back to your hut & relax. If anyone asks, you're on duty with me." Net result—3 hrs. of sleep this afternoon. I am in good with Lt. Levy alright.

You know, he's only 22—just a kid—happy-go-lucky, short, a trifle plump. Whenever you meet him alone outside of duty, his name is "Bob." A fine fellow.

Well, I'm on K.P. tomorrow, so better hit the hay. As ever

Bye

Love

Bud

In the present chapter, then, I will consider three themes represented in this early letter from Camp Blanding, analyzing the ways in which my father's beliefs about work and bureaucracy developed during his months in the army. First I will consider the basic concept of competence, tracing how my father came to understand himself as someone capable of doing good work. Next I will take up his growing understanding of—and occasional cynicism about—organizational hierarchy. Finally, I will examine the issue of my father's occupational choice by discussing his beliefs about the specific kinds of work that were best suited to him. In all three of these areas, I will consider social research that contextualizes my father's experiences within larger understandings of work and bureaucracy. The chapter will close by considering how my father's subsequent career continued the patterns established in childhood and in the army.

A Growing Sense of Competence

Perhaps the most basic aspect of learning about work is developing a belief that you are capable of doing the task set before you. This belief, "self-efficacy" in the language of social psychology,[2] has been connected to concepts such as motivation, psychological well-being, and empowerment.[3] Across a spectrum of social research, the development of a sense of competence is seen as an important aspect of individual and social growth.

As my father entered the army, he had mixed ideas about his competence. He clearly knew that he was intelligent—he had been very successful in school and rewarded often for strong academic achievement. The United States military, however, was vastly different from Urbana High School, and my father began his service with serious doubts about his soldiering ability. But early in basic training, he began to realize that he was surprisingly competent in soldiering tasks, including physical training and marksmanship. Most relevant to his understanding of work, however, was the extent to which he felt competent in his army assignments related to radio code and communications. As he slipped into these tasks, he quickly found that they were a good fit (March 7, 1944: "We had about 6 hours of code. I think I'm going to like it") and that he was pretty skilled. Three weeks later, he wrote home,

> *Well, I really surprised myself in code today. I passed 10 & am now working on 12. How do you like that? On 12 with me are 6 others—of those, 4 have had a little code or radio before the war. Practice at 14 sounds pretty fast, but the tests at 12 aren't bad. However, I don't expect to pass 12 till next week at least.*
>
> *I feel pretty good about the code.*

My father's sense of mastery in code continued as he worked his way past various "word per minute" benchmarks. At one point he reached a discouraging plateau, but still managed to feel reasonably good about his effort. On May 2, 1944, he writes, "Was trying to figure out why I seem to be at a standstill in code. Reached the following conclusion. I don't really have a talent for taking code, but on the slower speeds my powers of concentration & determination built up in school enabled me to pass fairly easily. Now at 16, where it takes natural ability to pass, I am lacking." However, he soon got past this plateau and finished his code training feeling quite competent in his status as a "20 W.p.m. man."

Dad also developed a sense of competence in other aspects of his work. As a member of the communications section, it was critical to take the basic tasks of sending and receiving code and put them to action in the field with radio equipment. A letter home on April 26, 1944, shows a sense of accomplishment in these tasks, as well: "We've been using the SCR 284 quite a bit in the last two days. Set up 4 station field nets, using 3 men on each set. Because of my speed, I was given an NCS each time—Net Control Station. Sure a lot of fun communicating with a guy a mile or two away. After today's 284 work Lt. Levy praised 2 men—me & Kreider. Both from Illinois naturally."

When my father moved to Camp Van Dorn and began work on field exercises, his belief in himself continued to build. On July 26, 1944, he tells his folks about a complicated exercise: "I really worked on that problem. I was in the message center most of the time. I didn't know much to start with, but I picked up quite a bit in the short time the problem lasted. I was code clerk—using the MZ09 & brevity code all afternoon and from 2 a.m. this morning till the problem ended at 10." In Europe, Dad was assigned to the message center rather than the radio unit, and he continued to feel good about his abilities in both areas. On February 6, 1945, he writes, "Sgt. Hassell has gone to a rest camp for a few days, so Brass & I are alternating on the desk at message center. In a way, I'm glad Jack went to rest camp—it gave me a chance to prove to myself I could hold down msg. cen. competently if the need arose." A few weeks later, after a transfer to the radio section, he writes on February 23, "I've found that I haven't lost my touch on the key despite an absence of several months from radio." Then, in the months after the war in Europe, he continues to express pride in his ability to get the job done (October 26, 1945: "Well, at least the film strip catalogue is out of the way. It turned out to be a pretty big job").

Thus, throughout his military service, my father's basic belief in his ability and intelligence was reinforced, and he also developed confidence in a wide range of specific tasks. This sense of competency was based, to a large extent, on successfully completing tasks and on hitting various performance benchmarks. In this his experience is consistent with the observations of social researchers like Albert Bandura, who find that the most important source of efficacy information is personal mastery of tasks, demonstrated through actual performance and accomplishments.[4] Similarly, Louis Cussella argues that individuals receive substantial feedback about how they are doing from the task itself.[5] But scholars suggest that there are also critical ways in which others in the social context contribute to the development of a sense of mastery.

One way this occurs is by comparing individual performance with the performance of others.[6] My father clearly made such social comparisons in assessing his competence in code. On April 13, 1944, he notes that he is "the highest man without previous experience," then provides the word-per-minute rates of all his buddies and concludes, "I guess I stand pretty high."

A second way the social environment contributes to the development of a sense of competence is through validation received from others. Abraham Maslow's classic hierarchy of needs theory divides the "esteem needs" into internal esteem that is achieved through a sense of accomplishment and external esteem that is achieved through public recognition.[7] Similarly, David Franks and Joseph Marolla distinguish between "inner self-esteem" based on efficacious action and "outer self-esteem" based on social approval.[8]

This process of looking to others for external validation was evident in my father's military experiences. At times validation came from official commendations such as graduation from basic training and code school or promotion within the army ranks. For example, when he was promoted to private first class on August 4, 1944, my father calls it a "pleasant shock" and says, "I guess that means I'm doing o.k., because several other men in my barracks who have been in the army longer than me, are still pvts." Later, when the table of organization was developed for shipping overseas, my father lets his folks know that he might take on the role of chief code clerk and get an accompanying promotion to corporal. He also appreciated being complimented by superior officers (May 5, 1944: "Brag department—Lt. Levy to Sgt. Jackson—'Miller set up the set better than any other man in the company.' Malloy overheard the above quote"). My father felt particularly good about himself when he was sought after by officers. On September 27, 1944, he writes, "Tomorrow Capt. Wright asked me to go down to Personnel to check records of the company with Corp. Grayson, company clerk. It seems everyone is after me now. Sgt. Dragon wants me to be a driver, Sgt. Pohlmeyer wants me to go down to battalion as a clerk, Kern still needs me in msg. center, & Larson is trying to get me transferred to radio. Oh, my!!"

Thus, life in the army provided my father with a general sense that he was competent in—indeed, pretty darn good at—a lot of tasks. He already knew that he was a smart kid. But through his steady performance on a wide range of tasks, through comparison with others, and through both informal praise and formal recognition, his sense of competence was reinforced and supplemented. Although my father sometimes had doubts about himself—and probably never thought of himself as a "good soldier"—his letters clearly reflect a sense of confidence in his ability to perform in all the tasks required of a member of the communications division during the war.

The Pains and Perks of Bureaucracy

> I also became something of an expert in writing citations for medals. This was really creative fiction. There was an awful lot of hustling for awards. Each one was worth five points. People were shipped back home in the order of points accumulated.
>
> ROBERT LEKACHMAN, IN STUDS TERKEL'S *The Good War*

Max Weber defined the bureaucratic organizational form as a system in which there is a clearly defined hierarchy, a strict division of labor, centralization of power, and a reliance on rationality.[9] Though Weber was a German sociologist writing in the late nineteenth and early twentieth centuries, his definition of bureaucratic organizational form clearly describes military organizations as they developed and were refined on both sides of the line during the first and second world wars. For the newly inducted, learning how to work in the army meant learning about the structures, rules, and systems that are inherent in bureaucratic organizations. My father was no exception to this necessity, and he quickly became familiar with the power structure of the army and with the red tape that kept it running.

An army private must contend with two sets of significant others within the military structure. At close quarters are the noncommissioned officers who have day-to-day control over activities and who work to "break down" and then "build up" the recruits. My father saw these NCOs as tough in his early weeks at Camp Blanding (March 13, 1944: "What a day! Officers & NCO's rough as the dickens today. Gave out gigs all over the place. Every man in our platoon gigged for something—NCO's saw to that"). Further up the hierarchy is an assortment of officers who have a significant degree of power and are seen as deserving varying levels of respect. Though my father occasionally derided those at the very top as "parade ground generals," he viewed officers further down the chain of command in a more favorable light. For example, on March 10, 1944, he writes home that Lieutenant Woods has officially taken charge of the company: "Everyone likes the new C.O. He's tough, but I've learned to expect that in everyone." Especially early in his army experience, there were times when he expressed awe, and perhaps fear, of those in power. On April 16, 1944, he writes home about his encounters with two officers:

> *Was on guard duty last night. Doggone, I had to draw the first post—around bn. h.q.—& did I get mixed up! Lt. Vogel, officer of the guard, came around inspecting about 7:30. I answered every question he asked to perfection. Then, about ½ hour later—*Major *Reaper stopped me. Gee, I looked at those gold leafs, & boy I got flustered. He started popping questions—I answered the first few—then he asked for the regimental O.D. I looked at those leafs again, got hot, &* forgot *the O.D.'s name. Well, I just hope Major Reaper doesn't report me. But I suppose he will.*

As he became accustomed to the power structure, my father also became intimately acquainted with the machinations of bureaucracy. In basic training, he coped with the process through which passes were assigned (February 26, 1944: "The captain [bless his soul] revoked all passes to the second platoon. The first & third got their passes, but *we* never got ours"), went through the motions of applying for Officer Candidate School (April 23, 1944: "All but about 10 men in the company put their names in. Of course none of us will go. In the last cycle, just 1 man out of 15,000 went to OCS"), and complained mightily about the red tape that kept him out of advanced code school at Fort Benning (June 5, 1944: "We were definitely 'rooked by the relentless ramrod of remorse.' Everyone says we were"). Dad became yet more intimately acquainted with the red tape in Europe, where he typed and retyped daily orders, requisition requests, and company reports. As he stayed on in Europe after V-E Day, he often joked about the time-consuming nature of often futile paperwork. On December 7, 1945, he writes: "Finally finished all my huge charts on the table of organization of the education branch. It was a pretty big job. Commended on it by Major Kates, but that is all the work will get me is a commendation. Eventually the charts will be thrown into the wastebasket in favor of a little more extravagant, a little more showy T/O."

My father's increasing familiarity with the military system bred mounting contempt, frustration, and even anger with what he considered the unfairness and self-serving cynicism of army bureaucracy. He saw it as excessively political, and he wrote home about incidents of brown-nosing, self-serving exploitation of the intricacies of regulations and the privileges of rank, and reciprocal back-scratching. At times Dad observed these deficiencies on a small scale. For example, he was repeatedly frustrated by the rating system through which individuals were promoted on paper in the table of organization, but did not actually receive a promotion. On October 21, 1944, a month or so before shipping overseas, he explains the problem to his parents: "I don't think I'll get my T-5 rating right away, after all. You see, all the excess noncoms we have in the platoon must be absorbed into the T/O. Sgt. Kern & Sgt. Herring have gone to OCS [Officer's Candidate School], but because the division is keeping rather than shipping excess noncoms, Sgt. Thompson (excess) is going to be msg. center chief instead of Brass. That means Brass will remain a corporal and I a pfc. Of course, the ruling may change—anyway I hope so."

In this letter from Camp Van Dorn, my father understood and accepted the situation. However, a year later he had seen enough of army bureaucracy to take a more jaded view. On October 5, 1945, he writes, "The jokers at the head of this program have dreamed up a new table of organization, and my new T/O rank is now Staff Sergeant. Ho hum—I suppose it will keep going up until some day maybe they will actually start promoting people instead of just having 'make-believe' non-coms."

On a larger scale, Dad lamented the unfairness of a system in which the "higher-ups" were motivated by the opportunity for recognition and advancement, and used those lower in the bureaucracy to achieve their goals. Very early in basic training (on February 27, 1944), he complains, "Everyone in the second platoon—including me—is still pretty mad over the raw deal we drew at inspection Saturday. Right now, I'm pretty firmly convinced that we trainees are just a bunch of numbers to the officers of the company. Those officers are interested solely in themselves. If they have to ruin a bunch of men to get a promotion, those officers will ruin that group of men." His belief that the army was too political persisted. At the close of the war in Europe, when he found himself typing up paperwork for battle commendations, he wrote (on May 7, 1945), "In spite of the fact that there is no more war over here, the army must go on. So I continue my work in the S-I office on awards. I don't think I'd take one of these awards if it were offered me, after the way I've seen politics affect the awarding. The only ones who get the Silver Star are officers, and the Bronze Star seems to be a matter of who does the most for the officers."[10]

My father's frustration with the unfair politics of bureaucracy became particularly acute when officers in post-war Europe who had never seen combat took advantage of battle-weary enlisted men waiting for their discharge point totals to pile up. On October 3, 1945, he writes,

It seems that the Captain "regrets" that conditions are so bad, but that everything possible is being done to improve them. Just like a damn Jap. He also

> *announced that effective tonight, I & E [information and education] men would have to start pulling guard at the billets, a duty which in all other Seine Section billets is strictly for MP's and billet cadre. . . . He said that he had been a billet commander for two years in TSFET now, and that the next few months would probably be the hardest we had ever spent or worked during the war. A rear echelon commando like that saying such a thing to a bunch of ex-combat men who have ducked more shells, mines, bullets, and bayonets than he ever saw.*

He goes on to contemplate the gratifying possibility of "repercussions" which might redound to

> *said captain and his miserable kowtowing staff of first and second lieutenants. The more I see of this army, the more I think it is run strictly on a political basis, with the best apple-polisher getting the best deal, and the enlisted men getting kicked out of them in the end. And I mean the end.*
>
> *Tsk, tsk, I shouldn't have blown up like that, but I am glad it is out of my system.*

But my father's ability to recognize the faults of the army did not sour him on the whole military experience. There were times when he felt great pride in his unit, beginning very early in basic training (February 10, 1944: "Convinced I'm in the best Co. in the Army") and recurring through his time in battle (March 23, 1945: "I've changed my mind about this division. I used to believe it wasn't much good, but now I think I'm really part of a crack outfit").

Dad's dislike of bureaucracy and of the REMFs ("rear-echelon motherfuckers")[11] who frequently staffed it neither blinded him to his good luck at having been put in a headquarters company and generally out of range of enemy fire nor prevented him from rather gleefully enjoying the uneven treatment of recruits when he benefited from it. For example, he thoroughly enjoyed being one of the platoon leader's favorites on March 27, 1944: "This morning Lt. Levy called out Kurt Pollak, Joe Moffitt, & myself to help him set up some TG's for a class he had later in the day. So we set them up in about ½ hour & then shot the bull for 2 hours while the rest of the company worked very hard—ha, ha, ha. The Lt. told us he had to talk 2 hours about a subject ('Message Center Procedure') which could be covered in 15 min. He said 'watch & see. I'll feed them a lot of bull.' And he did."

While he was at Camp Van Dorn my father also noted, on August 17, 1944, that ignoring bureaucratic structures and associated flatteries was common practice: "What continues to amaze me in our platoon is the complete disregard for NCO rank. Why, we joke with sgts. & corps. all the time, insult them, & have a lot of fun. Just today, while we were cleaning some EE8A's (field telephones to you), Leeton & I hooked some wire up to one, attached the wire to T-5 Brass's helmet—when he sat on the helmet, we turned the phone on—boy, what a hot seat!"

Later, after months in battle, my father found that good relationships could be forged in spite of the power distinctions dictated by bureaucracy. In a letter to his parents on June 16, 1945, he extols the virtues of his boss, sergeant major Arthur E. Pohlmeyer Jr.: "A finer man to work with could not be found. We work in coordination—there's no 'I'm your boss' attitude. He knows I can handle the sergeant major's job as well as he, so we both do about the same work. 'Pohly' always has a joke, is never out of humor, and never lets his job worry him."

Through his experiences in the army, then, my father developed somewhat contradictory ideas about bureaucratic organizations. At first glance, his position could be seen as organizational cynicism, which James Dean, Pamela Brandes, and Ravi Dharwadkar define as "a negative attitude toward one's employing organization, comprising three dimensions: (1) a belief that the organization lacks integrity; (2) negative affect toward the organization; and (3) tendencies to disparaging and critical behaviors toward the organization that are consistent with these beliefs and affect."[12] My father's letters home certainly sometimes expressed negativism toward the army, a belief in its lack of integrity, and willingness to share that belief, at least with some of his buddies and his family. Indeed, what evidently disconcerted him most was confronting hard evidence that "organizational actions [were] designed to further the ambitions of a few at the expense of many,"[13] a classic mark of a disillusioned organizational cynic. But my father also learned that valuable relationships which defy the organizational hierarchy can flourish in the workplace, and that the red tape, structure, and pettiness of bureaucracy don't always rule the day.

My father's contradictory attitude can be seen as self-serving, to the extent that he suspended his righteous anger over the evils of bureaucracy when he benefited from them, for instance through getting time for an extra bull session with his buddies or enjoying a preferred relationship with an NCO. It is also possible, however, to see this contradiction as a more nuanced understanding of power and politics in the organizational setting. Walter Davis and William Gardner maintain that work organizations are inevitably political entities, and that political machinations often lead to organizational cynicism.

However, these scholars also argue that cynical beliefs about power often depend on relationship quality such that individuals who have close ties with supervisors will be less likely to view differential behavior as political.[14] This seems to be one lesson my father learned about bureaucracy. He left the army highly cynical about structured organizations and the capricious ways power could be used in them, but with a clear understanding that relationships in the workplace are more important than the bureaucracy in which they are embedded.

The Right Kind of Job

> Though I was unable to shoot accurately and couldn't put one foot after the other in the right sequence, I could type. I was installed in regimental headquarters. I could write letters for people and hold their money and lose money in card games because I was a terrible player.
>
> ROBERT LEKACHMAN, IN STUDS TERKEL'S *The Good War*

Very early in life, children begin fielding the question, "What do you want to be when you grow up?" During childhood, this question of occupational aspiration is likely to provoke idealistic and unrealistic answers, but the fact that the question is asked and answered at all suggests that knowledge of occupational characteristics begins developing early in life. Contemporary scholars have investigated processes through which young people learn about occupational status and prestige, the responsibilities of various occupations, and the fit of an individual's skills and training with a specific occupation.[15] Not surprisingly, researchers have found that children and adolescents typically learn most about specific occupations from family members, educational institutions, and part-time employment.[16]

By the time my father entered the army, he appeared to have clear career aspirations—he wanted to be a journalist. It is likely that this occupational goal stemmed from the typical sources of family, school, and a part-time job. In 1933, when my father was eight years old, the unemployment rate in the United States reached 25 percent, and his own father was sometimes among the ranks of the jobless. However, as the 1930s progressed, my grandfather was able to find fairly steady work as a printer, and then eventually to buy his own shop. Dad learned about the printing business from his father, noting in his memoir that "I did some work in the shop, feeding the 10-by-15 or 12-by-18 press. Feeding a press requires a measure of dexterity and quick reaction times so you don't get your hand caught and smashed between the platen and the metal form. I did fairly well at it, but considered it pretty boring." This boredom probably ruled out the printer's trade as a career choice for my father, but his experiences at the shop may have provided a window into other career options related to the printed word.

At school my father excelled in all subjects, but he noted in his memoir that he found math boring. He was less bored, however, with English and social studies, and even with the classes related to the more technical cousins of writing. He reports that Sarah Jane Fisher was one of his favorite teachers: "Saran Jane Fisher taught shorthand and typing, and I was one of the few boys who took both. I was her star pupil." My father also gravitated to specific extra-curricular activities, including working for the school paper in both junior high and high school. His occupational aspirations were further nurtured in his part-time job as a sports reporter for the local *News-Gazette.* Thus, by the time he was eighteen, Dad had a clear answer to the question "What do you want to be when you grow up?"—he wanted to be a newspaperman.

My father grew up during an era when newspapers were an integral part of daily life. "In the early years of the twentieth century," George Douglas writes, "the daily newspaper was universally accepted as one of the foundation stones of American social life. In those days real authority flowed from the printed word, and the newspaper was clearly one of our most valued cultural institutions."[17] The importance of newspapers did not, however, necessarily translate into the desirability of journalism as a career. Fred Fedler says flatly that in the late nineteenth and early twentieth centuries, members of the upper class scorned journalists, seeing them as "poorly dressed and poorly mannered, heavy drinkers, prying, dirty, insensitive, rude, and dishonest."[18] Some of those associations persisted through World War II, and columnist Russell Baker disparaged his own career choice, observing that "in 1947 newspaper work was for life's losers. Men who dreamed of big money and rich wives went in for medicine, law, business, or engineering. Those like me, without talent for high-income work, might go to graduate school to become professors. . . . Newspapermen, by contrast, occupied the social pit."[19] Clearly, my father saw it differently. Perhaps, from the perspective of his bare-bones upbringing as the son of a printer, he saw journalism as a way to improve his life. Perhaps he saw it as a calling to inform the public and enhance the general good.[20] Most likely, however, he thought reporting was fun (especially sports reporting) and something he was good at.

So as he entered the army, my father had a view of his occupational future;

but how military service fit into these plans was another question. He knew very quickly that he wanted specialized training and was happy early on when he was selected for code class. On February 7, 1944, he writes home, "Will get 7 weeks straight basic training here at Blanding—then 10 weeks of radio. You have to be able to pass 13 words per minute at end of 13th week or you get transferred back to rifle company—so there will be plenty of work." A few weeks later (February 21, 1944), he again points out that only certain jobs within the army are a good fit for him: "Acting corporals appointed today. As they are squad leaders, they must be tall—which automatically eliminated me. All the appointees were guys 30 or over, too. Frankly, I don't figure to do anything outstanding in this outfit till we start radio code—some brain-work."

By the time my father shipped overseas, he was clearly grateful that his skills and training had kept him out of an infantry rifle company; this made a difference in many aspects of army life. For example, when he set off overseas on the Saturnia, he drew a stateroom with three other men in the communications division rather than a crowded room with rows of bunks. It is unlikely that soldiers in rifle units were so lucky. My father continued seeing such distinctions between the communications unit and others during the early weeks of battle. On January 9, 1945, he writes, "Right at present we've set up in an old schoolhouse. Message center, I believe, drew the principal's office. We set up there, & sleep in an adjoining small laboratory. We've got a stove, a couple desks & some candles, so compared to the line companies, we're living like kings." In short, my father had learned the army difference between regular soldiers and the "headquarters men," who, as Roger Little puts it, "were an elite group, having some attributes lacked by men of the line, the riflemen: either more years of education or service or more specialized skills."[21]

As the war continued, my father found himself doing work even closer to his adolescent aspirations. On March 12, 1945, he tells his parents, "I am now company reporter for 'Blood & Fire' division newspaper. It's just a little thing, involving my collecting one or two items a week about the men in this company and submitting them to the paper." Then, as the war came to an end, there were even more opportunities to exercise his journalistic bent. On May 3, 1945, he writes, "Beginning tomorrow, I'm going to be doing some work in the S-1 office—it's sort of a combination reporter, writer, and typist's job—getting facts of heroic deeds and typing them up to send in to regiment for consideration for awards." Two days later he extols the creature pleasures of this position, in which he now had an assistant: "We have an office to ourselves with two soft chairs, a desk, electricity, and steam heat. Enjoyable work."

It would seem, then, that my father's experiences in the army reinforced his ambition to become a journalist. He liked the work and excelled at it, especially in the confines of the infantry regiment headquarters company. After the war, he continued in clerical positions in Paris, Versailles, and Germany. At this time he was no longer part of an infantry unit, but instead found himself thrown in with a large number of headquarters men from across the military spectrum. He was quite impressed with the credentials and talents of these coworkers (October 3, 1945: "One of the men in the Art Department used to pull down 500 a week drawing a 'Jungle Girl' cartoon . . . and another guy in Art used to be an artist for the New York Times. And Howard, of the writing ends of things, was an associate editor of the New Yorker magazine"). My father enjoyed these relationships, but they also began to sow some seeds of doubt about his future career. On August 19, 1945, he confided his misgivings to his mother:

> *I've been thinking a lot, Mom, and have just about come to the conclusion that I'll never make a top-flight writer. I've read some of the stuff our average writers in the Public Relations department have written, and it seems to me that I just lack the imagination necessary to become an expert writer. I suppose I could hold down a fairly good job on a paper, and perhaps even become an editor in time, but somehow my ambitions reach higher than that. Newspapermen get paid very little, and are out of work quite often. If I decided to become a writer, I would want to eventually author a syndicated column, or perhaps write a few books. I feel that perhaps it would be wiser for me to go into business or law or something along that line. I believe if I did go back to school it will either be in the Commerce school or Law school. What do you folks think? I would certainly like to have your advice and ideas on the subject.*

It is interesting that my father saw a career in either business or law—both highly regarded by society at large—only as a fall-back position to his real career goals as a reporter, columnist, and writer. I don't know whether my grandmother offered any advice on the subject. But the fact is that on his return from Europe, my father joined the ranks of veterans taking advantage of the Servicemen's Readjustment Act of 1944, commonly known as the GI Bill, and majored in journalism.

War, Work, and Career in Context

In many ways my father's work experiences during World War II were typical of those of other young recruits. He was better educated, and perhaps smarter, than many young draftees, but he was still a green eighteen-year-old with doubts about his abilities. It is the way of the army to increase self-doubt in its recruits as it submits them to the physical and weapons and equipment training that exhausts them in body, mind, and spirit. But persistence at the training ultimately builds the men's endurance and capabilities so far from their starting point that they find new inner strength and confidence. This is what happened to my father as it did to many other young men. Peter Kindsvatter makes this point in his extensive study of combat troops in the twentieth century, noting that "soldiers who focused on their immediate responsibilities retained a sense of control over their situation, found that their actions made a difference, and took pride in their accomplishments."[22] And my father was also typical in gaining confidence from external sources: "The soldier's need for recognition was even more elementary than the desire for an award or promotion," Kindsvatter says. "He just wanted to be told that he was doing his share and that someone appreciated it."[23]

After the war ended, my father became part of the vast wave of men returning home to resume or begin education and work. Willard Waller, in his influential 1944 book *The Veteran Comes Back,* predicted that this reentry period would be disastrous because shell-shocked veterans would be unable to adapt to peacetime conditions.[24] However, Waller's predictions were not consistent with the mindset of returning soldiers, who largely "considered the "transition from war to peace to be a relatively simple process and were straightforward about their expectations."[25]

For my father, as for many returning vets, those expectations were to resume an education begun before the war. Michael Gambone observes that to "the young returnee in his late teens, school seemed an obvious choice, whether this meant finishing secondary education or moving on to college."[26] Indeed, with the help of the GI Bill, college classrooms were flooded in the fall of 1946 when my father showed back up at the University of Illinois. Gambone reports that the academic community had expected only a very small percentage of veterans to take advantage of the GI Bill's educational benefits, and "in April, 1946, when the Veterans' Administration reported that colleges and universities had provided 162,485 openings for veterans in the upcoming school year, there was a sense that the situation was well in hand."[27] It was not. More than two million applications flooded colleges that fall—almost half from veterans. These veterans also defied expectations that they would perform poorly in the classroom. "Much to the chagrin of their professors and many of their classmates, they became pacesetters in many courses."[28]

My father was one of these "pacesetters." He finished his journalism degree in three years and with perfect grades. Family lore has it that he wanted to go to law school, and that the need to support his mother and younger sister led him down the faster path to journalism. That story never rang true for me (my father a lawyer? It just didn't make sense), and the letter he sent to his mother about a career choice when he was close to returning home suggests that he never had a strong desire to attend law school. My father did not become a journalist out of expediency. Being a newspaperman was an integral part of who he was.

Though he never had to exercise his fall-back career options of law or business, my father's letter to his mother about his future occupation did prove prescient in other respects. He predicted that he could "hold down a fairly good job on a paper and perhaps even become an editor in time," and he was right about that. But he also worried that he would not be able to achieve his further ambitions—writing a syndicated column, perhaps a book—and he was right about that, as well. Though he had worked as a reporter during high school and college, he spent his entire career after graduation in editorial roles. His first full-time job was as a copy editor for the *San Antonio Express.* He then moved on to the now-defunct *New Orleans Item,* and soon received a more lucrative offer to work as copy editor at a prestigious Midwest paper, the *Detroit Free Press.* He took the offer, and spent the rest of his career with the paper affectionately referred to by many in Detroit as the "Freep."

My father worked at the *Free Press* from 1952 to 1982. He started as a copy editor, was promoted to chief copy editor (working "the slot"), spent a bit of time as state editor, then was one of two news editors for most of his career. His work involved editing stories produced by reporters, reviewing and editing wire service material, writing headlines and photo cutlines, and making decisions about the placement of stories in the paper ("dummying" the pages).[29] Some of this work was routine, but there were times when it involved substantial skill and creativity. He retired early (at fifty-seven), not because he didn't like what he did, but because he was burned out from the schedule and his daily commute. My father took great pride in his work throughout his career. My mother recently reminisced that he was "known for excellent newspaper work," and I believe this must have been true. He saw journalism as a craft and dedicated himself to doing it well.

Given his level of journalistic excellence, it is reasonable to ask why my father never rose further in the editorial ranks at the *Free Press.* I believe his experiences in the military provide some insight into his career path. While he was in the army, he had learned something about the power and politics of bureaucracy. But although he was not above enjoying the occasional uninvited perk that the bureaucratic system sent his way, it was nevertheless a system that offended him on both moral and aesthetic grounds, and he never learned or evidently tried to learn to manipulate it. In the newsroom of a large daily paper in the mid-twentieth century, he followed the same pattern that he had followed in the military. His interest and pleasure was in work and workplace competence, not workplace politics. My mother recently told me that there was "no niff-naw in him at all"—meaning that he was neither willing nor, probably, constitutionally able to engage in political maneuverings or self-promotion.

At age nineteen, then, writing from a desk in post-war Europe, my father had a pretty accurate view of his professional future. He was talented at newspaper work and was able to prosper throughout his career at a nationally regarded daily. However, as he predicted as a teenager, he was not destined to be a highly successful professional writer. He never abandoned writing (his letters to his daughters at camp were legendary), but when he tried to make a go of writing for pay during his retirement, nothing panned out. This did not, of course, negate his highly successful career in the newspaper business—a career that had its start when a shy boy walked into the *News-Gazette* sports department to ask for a job as a junior high stringer.

With the rise of the internet and the decline of advertising revenues, many commentators are now writing the obituary of the newspaper industry.[30] My father saw changes beginning in the last years of his work life—for example, he participated in the inevitable computerization of the newsroom. But he did not hear the current dire predictions about the industry or know that the *Free Press* would be the first large daily newspaper in the country to cut home delivery down to three days a week. Instead, he was a newspaperman during what were probably the last of the great years for American journalism. When my father retired, one of his colleagues worked a needlepoint wall hanging for him as a remembrance. It included a series of quotes from sources ranging from the Bible to Shakespeare to Walt Whitman to the Northwestern University fight song. The final quotation in the series (attributed to Anonymous) honors my father's anticipated retirement: "Hallelujah, I'm a bum." But the first quotation, from Byron, is a tribute to his working life as a newspaperman: "Let joy be unconfined."

CHAPTER SIX

Public and Private Morality

> A true war story is never moral. It does not instruct, nor encourage virtue, nor suggest models of proper human behavior, nor restrain men from doing the things men have always done.
>
> TIM O'BRIEN, *The Things They Carried*

THE CONCEPT OF MORALITY is complex. Morality can be understood descriptively, as a code of behavior accepted by any specific individual or group. In this sense, the Nazi Party and its followers had a particular morality during World War II. Or morality can be understood normatively, as a universal code theoretically accessible by a sort of natural law and acceptable to all rational members of society. It is generally understood as prohibiting behavior harmful to others, such as killing, causing pain, or deceiving.[1] Whether descriptive or normative, morality is typically seen as a code of conduct, or "a form of compliance that becomes part of the individual through the formation of, as examples, habits, conscience, or traits of character."[2] Some scholars have proposed that a moral code of conduct develops over a person's lifespan in identifiable stages. Lawrence Kohlberg's well-known theory of moral development proposes three major levels of moral judgment: a pre-conventional level in which individuals are guided by concerns with obedience, punishment, and self-interest; a conventional level in which moral decisions are based on social norms and concerns with formal systems of law and order; and a post-conventional stage in which people develop a more complex understanding of right and wrong, taking into account the competing interests of individuals and society.[3]

Thus, morality involves standards for behavior—ideas of "oughts" and "shoulds" that guide individuals in various life situations. These "oughts" and "shoulds" are often connected to social interaction and beliefs about others, as morality can dictate appropriate behavior toward others and is shaped by social comparison and social norms. Further, these "oughts" and "shoulds" can be codified into more abstract beliefs about right and wrong shared by large societal groups such as cultures or religions or held as individualized philosophies. Finally, the moral codes that guide behavior develop over time as people gain life experiences and come into contact with others who may influence their beliefs about behavior and standards of right and wrong.

In this chapter, then, I will consider the ways in which my father's beliefs about morality can be seen through the prism of his letters home during World War II, and the ways in which the war may have played a role in shaping his beliefs about right and wrong. In the first section of the chapter, I consider aspects of my father's moral code by first discussing his beliefs about appropriate behavior when he entered the war, then discussing ways in which those beliefs changed while he was in basic training and in Europe. In the second section I will consider the important role of the social system in shaping a moral code by discussing my father's beliefs about self and others as he encountered new people and places while he was a soldier. I will then discuss the extent to which these standards for behavior and beliefs about others were codified into more abstract beliefs about right and wrong, fairness, religion, and mortality. The chapter closes with a consideration of the ways in which my father wrestled with issues of religion and morality in later periods of his life.

"Thou Shalt Not": Codes of Conduct under Fire

> Mother always said, and Dad was the same way, "be nice to everyone." And we had a lot of bums come to the door, and we'd feed them, and they were very good about that even though they had so little. Being nice to everyone. The second rule was always wear clean underwear. And what else—never swear, never drink, never smoke [clears throat and laughs]—Sorry, Mom. I also cuss now!
>
> JUDITH MILLER PARSONS, INTERVIEW

In the childhood memoir my father penned after retirement, he writes often about his mother's attempts to instill concepts of right and wrong in her only son. These attempts were supplemented by lessons learned from other family members and from teachers, but it is clear that Irene Miller was the moral center of the family and the person who would administer punishment (most often spankings via hand or strap) if the moral code was violated. This moral code was based not on religious dogma but on more general principles (the golden rule) and on ideas about how good people (and, particularly, good children) should behave. As my father observed, "We never went to church and I never went to Sunday school. I don't recall there ever being any discussion of spiritual things. I guess there was too much in the way of practical things to talk about and argue about. However, Mom was adamant about teaching right from wrong, even though her methods proved rather painful to her son." These principles of right and wrong included general standards for morality ("to accept responsibility for my actions, to be truthful, to do assigned work on time") as well as more specific aspects of personal and social behavior, such as the "never swear, never drink, never smoke" admonitions mentioned by my aunt Judy.

Thus, by the time he entered the army shortly after his eighteenth birthday, my father's heartland upbringing in the home of Mr. and Mrs. O. F. Miller had provided him with clear standards for moral behavior. However, he realized within weeks of his induction that he was in the minority in adhering to some aspects of that code. Paul Fussell discusses the importance of drinking to soldiers, noting that "by the time of the Second World War, the notion that everyone has a perfect, even a Constitutional, right to a binge was thoroughly established in the United States."[4] Many of my father's comrades in basic training took frequent advantage of this "perfect right," and the word my father used most often to describe his attitude toward their drinking was "disgust." On March 19, 1944, he writes home, "I was never more disgusted at a bunch of guys than I was last night. Sgt. Putnam of our platoon was so plastered he couldn't walk home, & about half the other officers, noncoms, & men had jags of varying degrees." His attitude was unchanged almost two months later when he recounts, on May 8, "We sure had a mess of noncoms in the hut earlier this evening. Kreider, Hoover, & Pohlmann brought back a quart apiece of Old Taylor from Jacksonville yesterday—all 3 quarts are gone now. Disgusting, in my opinion." His opinion was not improved when he tried alcohol for himself: "Just got back from PX & Pepsi-Cola. Rest of the guys in the hut, drinking beer, induced me to taste it. I almost gagged on the stuff. I don't see how they stand it" (May 2).

In addition to refraining from drinking, my father was also determined during basic training to follow other "shalt nots" from his childhood. He attempted to obey his parents' admonition against profanity by setting up a wager with a buddy. On April 18, 1944, he writes home, "Steve & I have a bet on. Every time either one of us cusses we pay the other 5¢. Steve owes me 15¢ this far." A day later he notes, "Steve owes me 25¢ still. We're not doing much cussing." Presumably my father also refrained from smoking during basic training (and kept his underwear as clean as possible given army circumstances), thus adhering to the virtues instilled during his childhood.

Dad was disturbed when those around him violated his moral tenets. In addition to being disgusted at drinking, he became incensed—and heartbroken—when he became the victim of a theft several months after his arrival at Camp Blanding. On April 9, 1944, his letter home is angry (though it still largely avoids profanity):

> *I am very sick—at heart—right now. Remember I told you my watch was on the bum? Well last week I laid it up behind some letters on my shelf. Today I went to take it out to mail. It wasn't there.*
>
> *I have turned this place upside down—foot locker, clothes, barracks bag—everything. The fact remains, the watch is gone. It is quite clear that it has been stolen. I've reported the theft, but I don't suppose it will do any good.*
>
> *I don't believe anyone in my hut took it. I surmise someone wandered in during the day sometime last week when we were in the field—looked around, found the watch, and took it.*
>
> *Of course, the watch is valuable, but much more than the money value, I prize it because you gave it to me for my only graduation. I wouldn't have sold it for hundreds of dollars. And now some dirty damn sonofa______ steals it.*
>
> *Right now I don't care whether I get sent to a rifle company or not. In fact, I would rather like to be sent away from this thieving company.*

Dad continued to fret about the theft of his watch for several weeks. The next day he reports that announcements were made with no results, so "I may as well kiss the watch goodbye." The next day, he responds to a letter from home: "Hey, Dad, tell Tom he's lucky to get off with $19 lost—*I've* lost $45 watch. Still no sign of it." More than a week later, he holds out some hope: "Say, Dad—would you please go down to Frank's Jewelers right away, find out the serial number of my watch, & rush it to me airmail. Lt. Hoff called me in today and asked me to get this information as soon as possible." However, nothing came of this brief stir, and apparently Dad never recovered his "beloved tick-tock" and remained disheartened by the iniquitous standards that would lead someone to steal a valued watch from a fellow soldier.

But the strictness of my father's moral standards abated somewhat in Europe. With regard to alcohol, this is not at all surprising, as the stresses of battle, along with deepening relationships with buddies, could be expected to increase the odds of his learning to drink. "I drink very little," Bill Mauldin wrote, "and I don't like strong liquor at all. Yet there have been times over here when I have tied one on because I was homesick, or bored, or because I was sitting around with a bunch of guys who had a bottle, and when it came to me I just naturally took a belt at it."[5] I doubt that my father ever "tied one on," but he also didn't continue to feel the judgmental disgust that had colored his attitude about drinking during basic training. Less than two weeks after his arrival in Europe, he writes home that "I finally tasted champagne. It is not bad stuff. On the order of a sparkling wine" (December 21, 1944), and in the months that follow he talks about the ubiquity of alcohol (e.g., March 23, 1945: "Liquor very common around here—wine and harder stuff. They tell me some of it is pretty good stuff"). He still preferred Coke or Pepsi, but he didn't criticize those who washed down their meals with beer, champagne, or brandy. Indeed, during his final months in Europe, he participated a bit more in this GI pastime and even came to acknowledge that alcohol could play a role in enhancing social occasions (March 18, 1946: "I drank just enough champagne and sherry to make me bold enough to do some dancing with Bobby Dowling, Dick's girl friend. It was a wonderful party, and broke up about 3 a.m.").

In other activities, too, my father's moral standards moderated after he crossed the Atlantic Ocean. He encountered success in several poker games, attended risqué variety shows in Paris, and made some money selling cigarettes on the black market. All of these activities could be seen as violating the strict moral standards that he had grown up with in rural Illinois, and he was aware that the people who had been instrumental in developing those standards would disapprove. Thus, in writing home, he contextualized his behavior so that his parents (and later, just his mother) would see it in an acceptable light. For example, he describes a show at the Casino De Paris as "one of the highest class shows in Paris" (July 7, 1945), and he justifies his poker-playing with the comment that "we have nothing much to spend our money for," following up with, "I hope you won't think badly of me for doing it" (February 25, 1945).

Thus, after several years in the army, my father realized that the "shalt not" moral dictums imposed at home were less universal and less cut-and-dried than he had originally imagined, and he better understood the temptations of the larger world. After a trip to Brussels with his buddy Cy, he reports to his mother about the sinful pleasures available to soldiers on leave (November 16, 1945): "We were standing on Rainbow Corner debating which show to go to when a guy walks up to me and says, 'You want good drink, beaucoups young stuff plenty cheap—good girls?'" But in spite of such temptations, he still generally adhered to the morality of home; he followed up his description of the encounter on Rainbow Corner with a reassuring dismissal: "We just walked away from all propositions."

Will It Play in Peoria? Beliefs about Places and People

> Our impression of France, those of us who grew up in the thirties, was French maids, French poodles, a frivolous type of people. So it was striking to see these stolid peasants walking behind horse-drawn plows.
>
> ROBERT RASMUS, IN STUDS TERKEL'S *The Good War*

A central aspect of moral judgment and behavior involves relationships with others in a social context. In a basic sense, moral judgments often involve decisions about interaction with others (e.g., "Will my behavior cause harm to others?"). Beyond this, however, moral judgments are developed within particular social groups and settings. Descriptively, morality varies from context to context—what is moral in small-town Illinois may be different from what is moral in the Deep South of Camp Van Dorn, Mississippi, or in the mountains of Alsace during winter battles, or in postwar Paris. Even if we take a normative approach to morality that argues for a universal code of conduct, that code is still understood from the perspective of a particular social setting and position. Thus, an important part of understanding the development of morality is considering the ways that individuals understand the people, places, and situations with which they are confronted. These ways of understanding others may involve stereotyping, or generalizations or comparisons that may or may not be accurate.[6] The stereotypes can at times lead to prejudicial attitudes and discriminatory behaviors; or, they may be shattered as a person encounters people or places that explode previously held beliefs. All of these processes played out as my father moved from the confines of his childhood in Illinois to encounters with a wide range of unfamiliar faces and settings.

When my father entered the army, he had lived in several small towns in Illinois and in the somewhat larger college-town setting of Champaign-Urbana. He had traveled to Chicago and perhaps ventured outside the state to visit relatives in Terre Haute, Indiana. Given this limited experience, it is not surprising that he describes the places he encounters during his travels in the United States and Europe through the prism of a small set of geographical touchstones. Consider these descriptions of new places understood in terms of familiar ones:

- *June 4, 1944 (Jacksonville, Florida): "We left camp early—about 12:30—got to Jax about 2. It's a pretty big town—about the size of Peoria."*
- *July 16, 1944 (Baton Rouge, Louisiana): "Huey P. Long may have been a no-*

good so-and-so, Dad, but he sure beautified this town. The Capitol building he erected is 27 stories tall—a beautiful white marble building with a tower that lights up at night like Staley's in Decatur."

- *May 25, 1945 (Mannheim, Germany): "As a reward for being the assault battalion in the Siegfried, we got an assignment with army headquarters guarding installations such as factories in Mannheim. The city is of good size. About as big as Peoria."*
- *September 16, 1945 (Versailles): "Versailles seems like a pretty nice town. Rasmussen and I went in last night. It's a fairly good sized town, about the size of Champaign."*

These comments undoubtedly helped my father's parents appreciate his experiences, but were also critical in shaping his own understanding. In some letters he expanded his touch points to include additional places he had encountered more recently (e.g., comparing Brussels to Washington, DC, and the German countryside to Pennsylvania and Maryland), but throughout his letters he clearly had a U.S.-centric point of view. In telling his parents about crossing the Rhine, he notes on April 6, 1945, that "it's quite a little stream, but can't compare with some of our large rivers," and he corrects his sister when she suggests that his time in postwar France is enviable: "Doggone it, just because I'm living in Paris now is no sign I don't want to leave here. I would trade the whole country of France, including Paris, for our little town of Urbana" (August 22, 1945).

My father was surprised when encountering new places shattered some of his old stereotypes. He was clearly unimpressed with what he saw of France. On February 17, 1945, he writes, "The more I see of this country, the more I wonder why we don't let the Jerries have it. The villages are entirely unimproved. Each house has a pile of straw & cowdung in front of it. The bigger the pile, the more influential the owner of the house." My dad used these observations of village life to make inferences about French culture, as well: "The people around here, when they were here, that is,—led a simple life. No amusements or recreations are in evidence. I would say the people merely 'existed,' not 'lived.'" He was more impressed with what he saw of Germany. On March 22, 1945, he tells his parents, "For some reason, Germany so far is much more modern than I found France. Here the roads are better, towns more improved, and the homes on the better side. Then, too, there's not a pile of manure in front of every house as there was in France." My father, apparently, was not alone in his surprise about the living conditions in Germany. Stephen Ambrose reports that "the rural German homes had creature comforts—electricity, hot water, flush toilets, soft white toilet paper—such as most people thought existed in 1945 only in America."[7]

Not surprisingly, my father also relied on stereotypes in his descriptions of people he encountered during the war. His descriptions of his buddies often included terms that assumed an understanding of a stereotype, as when he described a soldier as "a typical college kid" or "a typical Jew." It's hard to know precisely what he meant by these descriptors, though it is likely that "typical college kid" was code for "a lot like me" and "typical Jew" code for "shrewd," "mercenary," "industrious," and "intelligent."[8] My father continued to rely on generalizations as he encountered new cultural groups in Europe. For example, he was not surprised when he and a friend found that the Louvre was closed when they stopped to view the art on a day off. He explains, "It seems that the caretakers of that gigantic place (three blocks long and a block wide), like all other Frenchmen, were lazy, and kept the place closed on Monday" (September 3, 1945). He speaks derisively of Belgians during his visit to Brussels (November 16, 1945): "One of the most revolting and disgusting things I saw was the way the Belgians seem to like a certain statue entitled 'Mannekeen Pis,' which portrays a little boy with no clothes on relieving his kidneys. It is in the form of a water fountain. . . . Very disgusting." He comments on the "entertainment and travel happy" nature of Parisians and commends the work ethic of Germans. He also lets his family know when he disconfirms a popular American stereotype during his trip to London: "And that old guff about the lack of a sense of humor—is just that—'guff.' We laugh at the same jokes, enjoy the same movies—although your English are a bit more conservative, I'll admit" (January 2, 1946).

Stereotyping serves an important role in social understanding and interaction. The generalizations that comprise stereotypes, though often woefully inaccurate, provide schemata that are useful in making sense of situations which might otherwise seem unfamiliar and strange. This process is especially pronounced during wartime: "Looking out upon the wartime world, soldiers and civilians alike reduce it to a simplified sketch featuring a limited series of classifications into which people, in the process dehumanized and deprived of individuality or eccentricity, are fitted."[9] Thus, my father simplified his world by referring to "typical Jews" and by categorizing Parisians as lazy and entertainment-happy, Belgians as disgusting, and the British as conservative. Like most soldiers, my father almost always used labels to refer to the enemy—opposing soldiers were "Jerries," "Heinies," and "Krauts." Further, terms that are highly offensive today occasionally found their way into his correspondence. For example, in describing his buddies in a letter home from Europe on March 4, 1945, he identifies Sgt. Art Bigger—A Chicago boy—called the 'Big.' Larson dashed off a poem which describes him admirably—to wit—

He's quite an electrical jigger,
This lad by the name of Bigger—
But his sartorial splendor,
Could be said to engender—
The tastes of a low class nigger.

Stereotypes were applied to self as well, as my father shed his boyhood identity and took on that of "GI Joe," a term that "completely expresses the utter anonymity of the private soldier."[10] In letters throughout training and in the ETO, he referred to himself as a typical GI with typical GI needs and desires (e.g., mail, packages, hot showers). And he was not just a GI, he was a member of the infantry, an identity description he shared with his parents on September 3, 1944, when he sent them the lyrics to a song honoring the stereotypical view of an infantryman as promoted by General Louis E. Hibbs. The lyrics ran, in part,

Give me my messkit and M1,
I just love a good squad run,
by the chiggers I'm bitten,
with GI shits I am smitten,
I am a combat soldier.

Stereotyping is the widely condemned practice of using mental shortcuts to assess people; it is also used to elevate groups to which we belong at the expense of groups to which we do not. It goes hand in hand with ethnocentrism and frequently results in prejudicial and discriminatory behavior.[11] However, there is an alternative view of stereotypes, namely, that they are valid starting points for understanding social groups and cultures. Psychologist Yueh-Ting Lee, for example, believes that stereotypes are necessary because they simplify processing information.[12] And there was much information indeed to process in the unknown and menacing world that my father and other young soldiers encountered during World War II. Stereotypes and ethnocentric views, however flawed, must have helped them impose order on that world and to make sense of previously unimaginable situations, thus, in Paul Fussell's words, enabling "sensitive people to survive the war relatively undamaged."[13] New understandings of others—in conjunction with codes of behavior developed early in life—also contributed to evolving beliefs about morality, mortality, and religion.

The Big Questions

> The awesome reality that we were training to be cannon fodder in a global war that had already snuffed out millions of lives never seemed to occur to us. The fact that our lives might end violently or that we might be crippled while we were still boys didn't seem to register.
>
> And if loyalty to your unit might ever seem an insufficient reason to fight the war, there was always the fall-back reason, which close scrutiny might expose as equally irrational: namely, to get home. To get home you had to end the war. To end the war was the reason you fought it. The only reason.
>
> PAUL FUSSELL, *Wartime: Understanding and Behavior in the Second World War*

One of my grandfather's best friends was apparently Argyle Hauser, a pastor at a Unitarian Church in Urbana. Hauser was the chaplain to whom Dad wrote soon after he learned of his father's death, noting both his own sorrow and the close relationship between Argyle and Oscar. Reverend Hauser was also mentioned in several letters written soon after Dad arrived at Camp Blanding in Florida. On February 16, 1944, he wrote, "Dad, tell Rev. Hauser I absolutely guarantee him a letter within the next 2 days. Also tell him I'd be honored to call him my pastor, for if I ever went to church, Argyl would be the boy for me." On April 6, 1944, he reiterated: "Tell Rev. Hauser I'd be glad to be counted a member of his church, if he wants a poor infantry private in such a fine organization." It is possible that Dad was just being polite and sending regards along to his father's friend. However, it is also possible that as Dad joined the army he started to contemplate some big questions about the war and what could happen to him as a soldier in the infantry. Though Argyle's church was probably not going to provide the answers, the thought of joining a religious organization might have started to have some appeal.

It is clear very early in my father's correspondence that his participation in the army was not motivated by desire to be part of a noble effort to rid the world of fascism. He was not driven by ideological ideals or patriotic fervor.

In this, he was like many other soldiers—surveys from the Army Research Branch during World War II found that most GIs had the primary war aim of getting home in one piece.[14] For my dad, this attitude was particularly strong as he reported to Camp Van Dorn in Mississippi. In the postscript to a letter written on July 12, 1944, soon after arriving, he recounts, "I was interviewed by the C.O. yesterday. He asked about my basic training, etc. He said to be frank, so when he asked if I liked the army I said no. He asked my main interest in the army. I said 'getting out of the army.'" His letters continued to reflect this "just get through it" attitude in subsequent days with comments such as, "Every time I turn around I curse this army & the war" (July 13), "I sure wish the Russians would hurry up & take Berlin & we'd take Tokyo, so this blasted war would be over" (July 14), and "I sure wish this war was over with," (July 16). A week later (July 23), he expresses some hope about the end of hostilities: "Well folks, it looks like the war is finally coming into its conclusive stages—the beginning of the end. This time next year I should be home. I know I can't be held in the army for more than 6 mos. after the war—& I figure the war will be over within the next 6 months." Of course, he was wrong in all of these assessments—he *could* be (and was) kept in the army for more than six months after the war's conclusion, and the war clearly was not over within the next six months. Instead, six months later, he found himself sitting by a camp stove at Camp Obberhoffen in France, preparing for battle.

During basic training, my father seemed to spend little time contemplating the dangers that might await him in Europe. He was evidently ready either to accept or not think about "the full, terrible implication of the term *replacement* in the designation of Replacement Training Center"[15] at Camp Blanding. He went through the requisite tasks of weapons drilling, code training, and combat exercises on bivouac, but—at least in his letters—he did not dwell on the fact that he was likely to be sent to battlefields where many thousands of young men had already died. My father had a small glimpse of possible dangers when a soldier from his platoon was injured returning from a training exercise. On August 8, 1944, he writes, "Everyone in the barracks feeling pretty rotten tonight because of an accident coming back from the field in which Dick Miller was seriously hurt—perhaps mortally. . . . Dick is in the hospital now with a broken hip, leg, arm, and as yet unknown internal injuries. At latest word from the hospital, Dick just got off the operating table, & his condition is getting steadily worse. As I said, we're pretty blue." The next day, he personalizes the accident, noting a fateful coincidence: "You know, about 10 minutes before the accident—before we started for camp—I was riding in that same jeep in Dick's spot—he was in another. Then we switched because he had all his equipment in the fatal jeep & I had mine in the other. Then came the accident."

Beyond this event, however, there was little in my father's stateside letters to show that he was cognizant of battle dangers and little to indicate that he was in the army for any cause other than getting through it. He was resigned to persevere and to "keep his chin up"—in short, to stay alive and out of trouble. He even noted that his rule-following nature would be instrumental in keeping him on the army's straight and narrow. He decided against sneaking home during a three-day pass because the military police might pick him up, although he sympathized when the second man in a week was found missing from the barracks. On July 14, 1944, he writes: "Frankly, I don't blame anyone from going AWOL from *this* camp. Everyone says it is absolutely the worst in the U.S.—& I agree with them. If the penalties weren't so severe, I'd be tempted to go AWOL myself. But of course I won't."

The reality of war hit my father in Europe. For most of his unit's time in battle, he was not in immediate grave danger, as the communications platoon was off the front line. But his retrospective diary reported often about the sounds of battle—about close calls with shells landing nearby or coming through the window or destroying a jeep, and about the wounded. The few times he was in more imminent danger, his diary suggested that he was cognizant of his mortality. For example, he reports that on January 26, 1945, "I was very scared," and on March 18, 1945, "Scared half to death the majority of time." But these fears were not apparent in his letters home. Paul Fussell argues that "one reason soldiers' and sailors' letters home are so little to be relied on by the historian of emotion and attitude is that they are composed largely to sustain the morale of the folks at home, to hint as little as possible at the real, worrisome circumstance of the writer. No one wrote: 'Dear Mother, I am scared to death.'"[16] My father's correspondence was no exception to this rule. Before shipping out, he adamantly tells his folks, "*DON'T WORRY!!!* Remember, I'll be in no danger" (October 25, 1944). While in Europe he mentioned possible danger only well after the fact. For example, on June 20, 1945, he confesses having been exposed to dangers only when they are several months in the past: "And once I was in a group strafed by an enemy plane—I was really scared that night—those bullets came too close for comfort. And on one occasion I was pinned down by Kraut machine gun and burp gun fire in a small patch of woods." In the midst of a battle, he reassures his parents with inaccurate probabilities and an appeal to a higher being he probably didn't believe in: "And, Dad—please try & avoid worry over me—just keep in mind the fact that there is a hell of a lot bigger person controlling our destiny than the Heinie who pulls the string on an '88.' Remember for every one that clips you for a wound, there are 1,000 close misses—and I have a long way yet to go on that thousand" (February 13, 1945).

My father's beliefs about the purpose of the war did not appear to change during his time in Europe. He still just wanted the war to end, and he wanted to go home. However, he was now motivated by more than his own personal desire to be reunited with his family in Illinois. In addition, he wanted the war over for the simple reasons that war was awful and that, though he might not be in grave danger, a lot of men were dying. On December 15, 1944, just days after arriving in Europe, he was incensed by a report about a U.S. Congressman who had recently returned from Europe: "Perhaps you folks read in the papers of Rep. Sheridan's ETO tour—how he failed to find a large number of GI's who wished to go home at present. In the opinion of every man I've talked to—and in the opinion of 'Stars & Stripes'—Mr. Sheridan is full of ______! Some of these bigwigs back in the States fail to realize that this war is no picnic—& that boys over here are certainly sick of war."[17] These feelings only intensified after three months in battle. On March 22, 1945, he writes, "Perhaps you folks don't think one way or another about the Germans. I, personally, though, have come to hate Kraut soldiers. It has been brought upon, I believe, by the sight of a few boys in the battalion whom I have seen killed. It really brought home to me what war really is—how dreadful and horrible it can be. Well, perhaps in the next few months this fracas will be brought to a conclusion and I can once more return to you folks. But some of my comrades will never return."

In the closing months of the war, and then during his time in post-war Europe, these changes in perspective seemed to coalesce into two overriding moral positions. The first, put simply, was that war is horrible. Part of this realization hit home viscerally when my father saw the utter physical destruction in France and Germany, and later in London (where he wrote, on March 12, 1945, "The devastation around here is certainly terrible—worse than at any other place I've been. In one town near here, I don't believe there is one good window, roof, wall, or house. Such destruction makes me very glad we're not fighting this war in America"). At times, my father experienced what Eric Leed described as the "radical discontinuity" of fighting in idyllic surroundings.[18] Contemplating the ruins of war in the midst of beauty reminiscent of an Illinois springtime led him to wax philosophic: It's a marvelous day today—sun shining brightly, the scent of spring in the air. Very remindful of spring at home—so much so that occasionally I fall into a daydream of home and am awakened by a burst of machinegun fire in the distance or the sound of a shell hitting. I sometimes wonder what ails mankind that two peoples—each enjoying the beauty of life—can think of destroying one another as they do" (March 14, 1945).

My father's second overriding moral conclusion—again, put simply—was that war is unfair. Its effects are felt differently depending on an individual's generation, nationality, and position. For example, as the war in Europe came to a close Dad ruminated on its implications for his age cohort: "Reading a letter over I got from John some time ago, I was struck today by the fact that our class has really scattered and disintegrated in the short space of two years. Three boys, I know, are dead—many others are in the Pacific or CBI, still others are over here, and a few lucky ones remain in the States. The blasted war certainly messed up a lot of good careers in that class" (April 29, 1945).

He also noted the differential effects of war on nations. On a trip to London, he writes to his mother on January 2, 1946, "I've decided that the people here had quite a lot harder time during the war than the Americans in the States. Whole blocks of the London East End are demolished, and a great many buildings in downtown London and the West End are badly damaged. And 238 women and children were killed here; and 194 here; and 342 here; and so on." And he even considered the inequities visited upon the enemy and made an early prescient comment about the future of nuclear proliferation. On August 9, 1945, three days after "Little Boy" was dropped on Hiroshima and the day Nagasaki was hit by "Fat Man," my father writes home, "You know, folks, I am almost sorry that this new bomb has been developed. I hesitate to think what might happen if that bomb got into the wrong hands. I am even a little sorry to hear of all those Jap women and children being annihilated by it. It's just too horrible an instrument of destruction, even to men hardened to killing and war."

Through the first eighteen years of his life, my father's moral code was shaped in straightforward ways by his parents and by the typical norms of the midwestern United States. Though his family was not religious, he learned many "oughts" and "ought nots" and took this moral code with him to basic training. He followed these rules on issues including drinking, swearing, and honesty in his own behavior and was quite judgmental regarding those around him who violated his standards of right and wrong. However, by the time he shipped back from Europe in April 1946, he had developed more complex moral beliefs. These came about in part through the natural process of maturation, but they were also shaped in profound ways by his contact with people and places very different from those he had known in Illinois, and by his experiences during stateside training, combat in the ETO, and his time in post-war Europe. Some of these changes were relatively minor, like the objection to alcohol that fell by the wayside in Europe. But larger changes in my father's moral beliefs came about as he developed more nuanced understandings of the people he encountered, of the nature and righteousness of war, and of his own mortality. In the remainder of this chapter, I will consider the ways in which these moral beliefs either persisted or shifted during the rest of my father's life.

Lifelong Wrestling with Morality

In *Flags of Our Fathers,* James Bradley describes the young men who were part of the famous flag-raising photograph on Iwo Jima: "They were nearly all poor. The Great Depression was a thread that ran through their lives. But then so did football, and religious faith, and strong mothers. So did younger siblings, and the responsibility for caring for them. And nearly all were described again and again as quiet, shy boys, yet boys whom people cared about."[19]

This description of the typical young World War II soldier could, except for one point, have been written about my father and his moral compass. He was raised poor with a strong mother to institute moral values. He had a sense of responsibility inculcated through family need and family values. He was a shy and quiet boy not quite ready for the wilder aspects of basic training and army life. His morality, however, did not come from religious faith but from a general belief in the goodness of people and in the importance of distinguishing right from wrong in dealing with them.

But like Bradley's father, my father—and his sense of morality—was changed by the war. His simple rules for right and wrong regarding individual behavior shifted as he encountered other soldiers who were not "quiet, shy boys." His early antipathy toward alcohol was tempered during the war, and by middle age a pattern of gin and tonics before dinner, wine with dinner, brandy after dinner had become routine; during retirement it became problematic. Thomas Childers writes of World War II veterans as "a silent generation" in which "big life changes—retirement, a death in the family, divorce—could trigger symptoms of PTSD, revise long-repressed traumatic experiences." I don't believe my father suffered from post-traumatic stress disorder, but it is possible that what he experienced during World War II—and his silence about it for many years after—played some role in his later-life problems with alcohol.

On the larger questions, too, my father's morality was shaped by war experiences. Soldiers, of course, have every combination of religious and secular orientation. There were religious soldiers in the war whose orientation toward God was a response to divine power. That power enabled God to decree the nature of morality, and thus to remain above it and outside it—one who delivered but was not subject to moral judgment. The creation was to be received on God's terms, by faith. The carnage of war did not threaten to unseat the god of soldiers who took this view. J. Glenn Grey, who distinguishes between different types of morality on the battlefield, termed such god-centered soldiers "other-worldly."[20]

On the other hand, there were religious soldiers whose orientation toward the divine was a response to its perceived goodness; their religion was social and ethical in content, and it was in that sense humanistic and "this worldly." These soldiers worshipped a god whose principal requirement of humanity was goodness, and whose actions seemed, therefore, like humanity's, subject to moral judgment. And these were consequently the soldiers who "often [found] the war's destruction wreaking havoc with their belief"—in God and humanity alike.[21]

My father was a secularist who was nevertheless concerned with the nature of the god he could ultimately not help rejecting. He did not enter the military with religious convictions about salvation or about a god who took sides in military conflict. He did, like the this-worldly soldiers whose moral values he shared, experience war as a possible disconfirmation of humanity's goodness. In its destructiveness war seemed inconsistent with human goodness, and it promised to be even worse in an atomic future.

For my father, though, the end result of war experience was not a rejection of this-worldly values. It was instead a lifelong questioning of the other-worldly thinking that centered on notions about faith and salvation. Though my mother sometimes persuaded my father to attend church with her (for short periods early in their marriage, and occasionally after retirement), he was never comfortable either with the social aspects of church or with its elevation of faith over this-worldly morality, when the principal discernable virtue of faith was its supposed ability to achieve salvation for those who possessed it. This lifelong conundrum culminated eventually in a book-length manuscript, "In the Image of Man," that provided a sometimes humorous take on religious issues, and in short writings during his retirement. In one of these musings, he describes a placard he had seen in a televised World Series game. It read, "EPH 2/8–9." He looked up the verse ("For by grace you have been saved through faith; and this is not your own doing, it is the gift of

God—not because of works, lest any man should boast") and then wrote, "And that is one of the sticking points on which I have argued with Margaret in the past. We don't argue about religion any more because it gets us nowhere—we have agreed to disagree, and do so quite amicably. It seems to me that if 'works' have nothing to do with salvation—that faith alone counts--there is a disincentive for a person to be concerned with 'works.' In other words, 'Why should I go out of my way to do good works and try to improve the neighborhood, the community, the world, when God cares only about faith?'"

Lawrence Kohlberg's theory of moral development argues that there is an ethical stage in which individuals move beyond the laws and rules of such social systems as governments and religious organizations, to consider morality based on universal standards of justice. Kohlberg's emphasis on justice has been critiqued by theorists such as Carol Gilligan, who suggests that an alternative form of moral reasoning should be based on the concepts of compassion and caring.[22] By the end of his life, my father's moral code had moved far beyond the "oughts" and "ought nots" of his childhood and had come to embrace moral principles like those of both Kohlberg and Gilligan, who assert the values of both justice and compassion as demonstrated through the behaviors of responsibility and good works. Further, his moral code rejected many religious formulations of morality—he did not consider belief, obedience, and mere faith virtues. My father—intelligent and rational man that he was—reached these conclusions after extensive reading, deep thought, and long conversation, and he expressed the ideas clearly and conclusively. In the end, he settled on a "this-worldly" morality and firmly rejected an "otherworldly" one.

However, I am not sure my father was ever totally at peace with his conclusions. He argued in many forums about his rejection of the concept of salvation, but I believe he also felt an emotional pull toward that very idea. My mother recently told me that on several occasions he said to her, "I want what you have," and "I want to know what you've got." The reassurance my mother derived from her religious beliefs was appealing to my father, but he just couldn't bring himself to participate wholeheartedly in a system that had not withstood his rational investigation and that he moreover found hypocritical. As my mother concluded, "he really wanted it—he was just too honest with himself to accept it."

These struggles came into sharp relief in 1978, when he learned that my oldest sister, Mary, planned to quit her job as a journalist with the *Grand Forks Herald* in North Dakota and attend Methodist seminary at Boston University.

She was leaving his beloved institution of journalism for a career that he held in very low regard. When I recently asked my mother about his reaction to her decision, Mom's response was forceful: "He was devastated." She went on, telling me he believed that Mary was going to "throw away everything she knows"—everything he had taught her—"to be a charlatan." Several days later, my father wrote Mary a long letter in which he discussed his beliefs about religion, questioned her motivation for going into the ministry, and argued that an individual can do more good works as a journalist than as a minister. At the end of the letter, though, he tells her that "the moral of all this—and this will shock and surprise you, no doubt—is that I think you should do what you think best. If you really and truly believe that the ministry is for you and you will find the best of lives in it, go to it." My sister did, indeed, do what she thought best—she attended seminary and was ordained into the ministry. My father came to accept this choice, though he would often instigate discussions in which he could pointedly contrast his views of religion with hers. In the end, though, I believe he realized that her rejection of journalism was not a comment on its value or on his own career choice. Instead, he saw that she was simply finding an alternative avenue for enacting the central features of his own moral code—respect for others, compassion, and good works.

A Reluctant Member of the Greatest Generation

> "The Greatest Generation is more invention than truth, and the consequences of such an invention, even one as attractive as this one, are far from harmless."
>
> KENNETH D. ROSE, *Myth and the Greatest Generation*

According to *Publisher's Weekly,* Tom Brokaw's book *The Greatest Generation* was the number two nonfiction bestseller in 1998 (bested only by Suze Orman's *The Nine Steps to Financial Freedom*).[1] In 1999, *The Greatest Generation* again made the number two spot on the list (this time bested by Mitch Albom's *Tuesdays with Morrie*), and Brokaw's follow up to it, *The Greatest Generation Speaks,* was in the number seven spot. His third book, *An Album of Memories,* came along two years later. In these books, which have "essentially become a branded item,"[2] Brokaw argues that the World War II generation can rightfully be called the greatest generation that America has ever seen.[3] In his introduction to the first book, Brokaw describes the hallmarks of that generation:

> *These men and women came of age in the Great Depression, when economic despair hovered over the land like a plague.... They had learned to accept a future that played out one day at a time. Then, just as there was a glimmer of economic recovery, war exploded across Europe and Asia.... They answered the call to help save the world from the two most powerful and ruthless military machines ever assembled.... They faced great odds and a late start, but they did not protest. At a time in their lives when their days and nights should have been filled with innocent adventure, love, and the lessons of the workaday world, they were fighting, often hand to hand, in the most primitive conditions possible.... When the war was over, the men and women who had been involved, in uniform and in civilian capacities, joined in joyous and short-lived celebrations, then immediately began the task of rebuilding their lives and the*

world they wanted. They were mature beyond their years, tempered by what they had been through, disciplined by their military training and sacrifices.[4]

In the years since those books were published, Brokaw's concept of the Greatest Generation has gained wide cultural acceptance and considerable political potency. Rod Gragg echoes Brokaw's sentiments in a 2002 compilation of letters sent home by soldiers during the war. He raises a paean to their service and their willingness to render it: "Fueled by the patriotism, discipline, and sense of duty that typified their generation, they put aside their civilian lives and put on their country's uniform."[5] Tom Mathews considered the challenges of the Baby Boom generation in his book *Our Fathers' War: Growing Up in the Shadow of the Greatest Generation,*[6] and, not surprisingly, when the World War II memorial was opened, the ceremony was entitled "The Greatest Dedication." The term has fueled much political discourse in recent years. Denise Bostdorff commented on the comparisons that were made between World War II and terrorism in the days following September 11, 2001: "When the attacks came, parallels were immediately drawn between the threats faced by the World War II generation and the younger generations. Television commentators talked about the attacks as another Pearl Harbor, as did political figures interviewed by the press. Repeatedly, news stories quoted young people referring to September 11 as 'our' Pearl Harbor or 'our defining day.'"[7] George W. Bush appreciated this juxtaposition, and his address to the UN General Assembly in November 2001 provided parallels between contemporary times and those of World War II : "We did not ask for this mission, yet there is honor in history's call. We have a chance to write the story of our times, a story of courage defeating cruelty and light overcoming darkness."[8] The romance of the Greatest Generation clearly infected the general public as well, and it continues to hold sway. Indeed, on several occasions when I told people about the book I was writing, their immediate response was, "Oh, you're writing something like Tom Brokaw and the Greatest Generation."

Some commentators have argued, however, that the concept of a "Greatest Generation" mythologizes both World War II combat veterans and those who persevered on the home front. Even in the first book, Brokaw cites Andy Rooney—a reporter for *Stars and Stripes* during the war and longtime curmudgeon on *60 Minutes*—as objecting that there was nothing special about those born in the 1920s—that instead, through the vagaries of history, "his generation had a Depression, World War II, and a Cold War against which to test their character."[9] Scholars have also forcefully argued that our idealistic construction of the Greatest Generation should be countered with a more careful consideration of how our views of World War II have been created and sustained. Kenneth Rose says that "if we approach this conflict through the historical record, rather than through a mythological creation, what emerges is a more subtle, that is to say more human, portrait of Americans at war."[10] Thomas Childers further cautions against the easy dangers of idealizing the Greatest Generation: "This glowing homage has become more than tribute to a passing generation; it has become our public memory of the war and its aftermath, a quasi-official transcript of events that glides sentimentally over what for many veterans was a deeply troubled reentry into a civilian world that, like themselves, had undergone dramatic change."[11]

Not surprisingly, the mythologizing of "the good war" and the Greatest Generation began during the war. "The selective process by which only positive aspects of the war received mainstream attention began during the conflict itself—one of the most censored events in modern history."[12] This manipulation of the facts of the war was taken up by official government censors, by war reporters who didn't want to shock civilians, and by members of the entertainment industry who presented glamorized film views of the war that were "a winning combination of escapism and toe-tapping patriotism."[13] The construction of World War II as a "good" war and the heroizing of all those who participated in the war effort continued in part because the public learned more about the atrocities that had occurred in Nazi Germany and Japan. However, there was also a need to create a compelling narrative for America that would allow its citizens both to feel good about and to move beyond the global conflict. Indeed, given the sanitized depictions of World War II, it is small wonder that soldiers in Vietnam were shocked to discover how little the fighting in a real war resembled John Wayne's depiction of it in *Sands of Iwo Jima.*[14] Nevertheless, for good or ill, World War II "has been converted over time from a complex, problematic event, full of nuance and debatable meaning, to a simple, shining legend of the Good War. For many, including a majority of survivors from the era, the war years have become America's golden age, a peak in the life of society when everything worked out and the good guys definitely got a happy ending. It was a great war. For Americans it was the best war ever."[15]

Two of the most notable opposing voices have belonged to novelists. James Jones in 1962's *The Thin Red Line* and Norman Mailer in 1948's *The Naked and the Dead* offered more nuanced views of the war.[16] Historians, too, including Michael C.C. Adams, Kenneth Rose, Thomas Childers, and Gerald Linderman, have written books attempting to provide a more accurate view of many aspects of the war, including the nature of combat and also racial tensions, war profiteering, and the problems of returning veterans.[17] Their social histories invite readers to "see incompetence, racism, greed, and brutality amid a wartime generation celebrated for self-sacrifice, unity, and patriotism."[18] Similarly, Studs Terkel, quoting voices from the fronts and from home in his oral history of the war, places ironic quotation marks around *"The Good War"* of the book's title.[19] And numerous memoirs cast a jaded eye on the experiences and the aftermath of the conflict.[20] Perhaps the writer who has most forcefully brought home the point that World War II should not be viewed through rose-colored glasses is Paul Fussell,[21] a cultural and literary historian among whose many books are three dealing specifically with World War II. The first of these is a well-regarded social history, *Wartime: Understanding and Behavior in the Second World War,* published in 1989. Fourteen years later, in *The Boys' Crusade,* Fussell concentrated specifically on the infantry battles in northwestern Europe during 1944 and 1945. I have relied on these sources often in previous chapters. Sandwiched between the histories is Fussell's 1996 autobiography, *Doing Battle: The Making of a Skeptic.* In that book he tracks the development of his critical, even cynical social views, from their beginning in his early childhood in Pasadena, through his military service in World War II, and into his career as an academic and social critic. In all these books, Fussell contrasts his own wartime experience with the sanitized versions of the war that have found their way into the culture.

As I read *Doing Battle,* I found myself comparing Paul Fussell's life and experiences with my father's. There were both notable similarities and important differences. Fussell and my father were born only twenty months apart; they were both children during the Great Depression and were both raised by parents with strong moral standards. Fussell grew up in a household whose "tone was that of Midwestern uprightness, and the rules were plain: do not smoke, or drink, or swear, or gamble; attend church; pay your bills immediately; work hard; tell no lies; succeed—and never buy anything on the installment plan."[22] Both Fussell and my father had an early love for the printing press, and both entered college intending to go into journalism. They began their military service within seven months of each other. Both went through stateside training with the hope that the war would end soon, but, instead, both shipped out at the end of 1944 and landed in Marseilles. Both saw their first combat in the Vosges Mountains of the Alsace region of France. Both received Bronze Stars. And both remained in the Army after the end of hostilities (my father in Europe, Fussell stateside) and were discharged in the spring of 1946.

But Fussell was brought up in an upper-class neighborhood in Pasadena, quite unlike my father's rural Illinois. Fussell's father was an attorney—formal, dignified, and highly respected for his material success—while my grandfather was an intermittently employed printer who loved hunting, fishing, baseball, and bad puns. Fussell served in the military as an officer—a platoon leader in an infantry rifle company, while Dad, though also in the infantry, was an enlisted man working in the communications platoon of a headquarters company. Fussell was injured in the war, my father was not. And though they both took advantage of the GI Bill to continue their education after the war, my father stuck with journalism, while Fussell earned his PhD in English from Harvard and went on to a highly productive academic career.

So Fussell and my father started life in different ways and ended it in different ways, but they both defined themselves—although to different degrees—in terms of the great experience of their generation, which they shared. Fussell emerged angrier than my father—he was more skeptical and more cynical, and I think the war cast a longer, darker shadow over his life than it did over Dad's. In a way Fussell never managed to extricate himself from the war, and my father did. But my father did not reject the experience. Perhaps he compartmentalized it. He saved the letters, the medals, the uniform, and assorted other mementos from that period of his life. It was a part of his life that he wanted to memorialize, if not necessarily to talk about.

When my father returned from Europe in the spring of 1946, the country was well past the triumphant parades and proud homecomings. Paul Fussell talks about wiring his parents the news of his discharge with the simple statement "GOT OUT," and then meeting them at the train station for the drive home.[23] Though my father's letters about being discharged were more enthusiastic, his arrival home was lonelier than Fussell's and bereft of celebration. He told my mother that he walked home from the bus station and found an empty house—everyone was at work or school. Though he was disappointed by this anticlimactic moment, it was a fitting start to the many years in which he moved ahead in life with very little looking back at his wartime experiences. He talked little to my mother about his war years—indeed, when he died, she was still pretty sure that he had spent part of his overseas time in Italy. And though all his daughters knew that he had been in the war, none of us took much initiative to ask him about it when we were growing up. We evidently felt little curiosity about the war and insufficient respect for his part in it. I still cringe at the memory of finding his army fatigue jacket as a teenager, thinking it looked pretty cool, and wearing it around the house for several days. If Dad thought this was as insensitive as I now believe it was, he never said so.

But his silence about his experiences in the war eased in later years, after his retirement. I remember looking at the wartime diary that I have quoted extensively in this book, and asking about some of its entries. He would expound on the joy he had felt at getting to bathe after many days, but not on how scared he had been at the front line. And though the letters he sent to his daughters while we were away at summer camp were celebrated, it wasn't until he was writing to granddaughter Katie at Camp Whispering Wood that he saw fit to mention his own "camp" time at Camp Blanding and Camp Van Dorn: "Basic training was unpleasant at times, but I did learn some useful things, like how to use a bayonet. The idea is to run the bayonet through a straw figure and shout, 'EEEYAAH.' Fortunately I didn't have to use a bayonet when I was in combat in Europe. Pretty messy. I also had to take a 25-mile overnight hike and a 9-mile speed march. Hut-hut-hut. Hot-hot-hot." He then goes on to tell Katie a bit about Camp Van Dorn and shipping off to Europe, closing with the comment, "Some day, maybe, I will tell you about my experiences there." I'm not sure that he ever did, but the offer suggests that he was thinking much more about his army experiences in later life.

For several years in the mid-1990s, I taught at the University of Kansas and lived in Lawrence with my family. At one point during that time, Dad and I spent a day driving to Abilene to see the Eisenhower Presidential Museum. The majority of the museum is devoted to what many see as Eisenhower's most important contribution to the nation, his role as commander of troops in the ETO during World War II. The few hours in that museum were among the most precious I ever spent with my father. He was never much of a talker—especially not about the war—but as we moved through the displays, he shared both his general knowledge of the war and some insight into his own experiences. He showed me which guns he had trained on, pointed out the kind of radio he had carried on his back, and stood in front of a battle map tracing his locations during critical battles. During the two-hour drive back over I-70, we kept talking. It was the longest conversation I ever had with Dad about the war, and though I don't remember the details, I do remember my sense of being honored that he was sharing those memories with me.

So at the end of his life, did my father see himself as a member of the "Greatest Generation"? I don't really think so. My mother doesn't remember his ever reading Brokaw's books, but I'm quite sure that he would see himself as a bad fit for many of Brokaw's generalizations about the GIs who fought the war. Across the interviews, letters, and narratives in the Greatest Generation books, several themes are apparent: members of the Greatest Generation believe in personal responsibility (my father would agree); members of the

Greatest Generation have great love of country and a strong sense of patriotism (my father would both agree and disagree); members of the Greatest Generation appreciate hard work and the value of a dollar (my father would agree); members of the Greatest Generation have an abiding faith in God (my father would clearly disagree). In all, a mixed bag, pointing to the obvious fact that though some generational patterns can, perhaps, be identified, the Greatest Generation is often depicted more as a caricature than a portrait. Indeed, at the end of his life, my father was a staunch opponent of the Iraq War, and he had an abiding enmity toward George W. Bush. I am not sure whether he was aware of all the comparisons made between the Iraq War and World War II, between 9/11 and Pearl Harbor, between Saddam Hussein and Hitler. I do know, however, that the simplicity of these comparisons would have offended him. He would not want have wanted his experiences twisted into a justification for a war he believed was wrong.

Conversely, I don't believe my father would say that his experiences as a young adult made him a total cynic toward war and government institutions. During the Vietnam War, his attitudes were those of much of the nation—supportive at first, then shifting as the war dragged on. Further, I don't believe he felt righteous anger toward institutions of public life—merely bemused frustration. So though the war did not make my father a card-carrying member of the Greatest Generation, neither did it make him a skeptic. It is interesting to note that in the last few pages of *Doing Battle,* Paul Fussell points to several ways in which he is perhaps less skeptical than his earlier writing would suggest. For example, he notes that "despite some of my critical views about America, the very idea of the Constitution moves me, for there's an implication in it of the essential decency of ordinary people who make up the electorate, crazily as they may behave on occasion. That implication, however false, does honor to human nature and to the admirable hope that people will act justly and wisely if given the chance."[24]

These are sentiments that my father could believe in—convictions that echo many of the conclusions reached in previous chapters about the kind of man he became. With his belief in free will, he knew that people would often mess things up, but he also knew that compassion and love would just as often lead to good outcomes. He believed in the importance of personal responsibility—of accepting the need to act justly and wisely. He believed in the importance of connections to others—even if he sometimes found those connections difficult to establish and maintain. He was frustrated by bureaucracy, politics, and red tape, but he believed in the essential rightness of the values on which America was founded, and he knew that American institutions—

especially the press—were essential to upholding those values. These beliefs were much more nuanced than the clear-cut values often attributed to the Greatest Generation, but they were shaped by the experiences shared by the members of that generation. My father's life was not determined by the Great Depression or World War II. But the boy who was Bud would have become a very different man had he not been a part of that history.

NOTES

PROLOGUE

1. Paul Fussell, *The Boys' Crusade* (New York: Random House, 2003), 6–7.

2. Robert Kotlowitz, *Before Their Time* (New York: Anchor Books, 1997), 4.

3. Fussell, *Boys' Crusade,* 7–8.

4. The Oxford Companion to American Military History, ed. John Whiteclay Chambers (Oxford: Oxford University Press, 1999), 849.

5. Glen H. Elder Jr., "War Mobilization and the Life Course: A Cohort of World War II Veterans," *Sociological Forum* 2 (1987): 453.

6. Robert J. Havighurst, John W. Baughman, Ernest W. Burgess, and Walter H. Eaton, *The American Veteran Back Home: A Study of Veteran Readjustment* (New York: Longsman, Green, 1951), 188.

7. Elder, *War Mobilization and the Life Course.*

8. Ibid., 463.

9. Quotations from my father are from the following sources in the family archives and are cited in the text: (1) correspondence with his parents and daughters; (2) a handwritten diary dated 1945; (3) a 56-page memoir in typescript written in the 1980s; (4) "In the Image of Man: What Religion Is All About or at Least What Religion Ought to Be All About," an unpublished 191-page novel in typescript from 1988; and (5) notes written after his retirement.

10. See, for example, Bill Adler with Tracy Quinn McLennan, eds., *World War II Letters* (New York: St. Martin's, 2002); and Andrew Carroll, ed., *War Letters: Extraordinary Correspondence from American Wars* (New York: Washington Square, 2001).

11. Herbert J. Obermayer, *Soldiering for Freedom* (College Station: Texas A&M University Press, 2005).

12. Studs Terkel, *"The Good War": An Oral History of World War II* (New York: New Press, 1984).

13. Susan Faludi, *Stiffed: The Betrayal of the American Man* (New York: HarperCollins, 1999).

14. Debra Umberson, *Death of a Parent: Transition into a New Adult Identity* (Cambridge: Cambridge University Press, 2003).

15. Norman K. Denzin, *Interpretive Biography* (Newbury Park, California: Sage, 1989), 13.

16. Ibid., 17.

17. Nick Trujillo, *In Search of Naunny's Grave: Age, Class, Gender, and Ethnicity in an American Family* (Walnut Creek, California: AltaMira, 2004).

18. H. Lloyd Goodall, *A Need to Know: A Clandestine History of a CIA Family* (Walnut Creek, California: Left Coast, 2006).

CHAPTER ONE

1. Russell Freedman, *Children of the Great Depression* (New York: Clarion, 2005), 14.

2. Herman J. Obermayer, *Soldiering for Freedom: A GI's Account of World War II* (College Station: Texas A&M University Press), 12.

3. Ibid., 50.

4. Don Pfeiffer, *IRTC Handbook: Camp Blanding, Florida* (Camp Blanding, Florida: Special Service IRTC, n.d.), 5.

5. Ernie Pyle, "The God-Damned Infantry," *Reporting America at War,* PBS, accessed November 18, 2009, www.pbs.org/weta/reportingamericaatwar/reporters/pyle/infantry.html.

6. Earl Wavell, "In Praise of Infantry," *Times,* April 19, 1945.

7. "Army Battle Casualties and Nonbattle Deaths in World War II," HyperWar Foundation, accessed January 12, 2010, http://ibiblio.org/hyperwar/USA/ref/Casualties/index.html.

8. Pfeiffer, *IRTC Handbook,* 2.

9. Robert S. Rush, *GI: The US Infantryman in World War II* (Oxford: Osprey, 2003), 35.

10. Ibid, 29.

11. "Boloed" means failed to pass the marksmanship test.

12. "History," Van Dorn Army Museum, accessed November 18, 2009, http://www.vandornmuseum.org.

13. L. M. Caulfield, *Birth and Death of a World War II Army Camp—Camp Van Dorn, Mississippi,* 63rd Infantry Division, accessed November 18, 2009, http://www.63rdinfdiv.com/historyvandornpage2.html.

14. Ibid.

15. Ray Wax, in *"The Good War": An Oral History of World War II,* by Studs Terkel (New York: New Press, 1984), 301.

16. Harris Peel, *The Trail of 254 thru Blood & Fire* (Gopingen, Germany: J. Kirchner, 1945), 3.

17. Ibid.

18. James E. Hatcher, *Blood and Fire: With the 63rd. Infantry Division in World War II* (n.p.: 63rd Infantry Division Association, 1986), 5.

CHAPTER TWO

1. Of all those mentioned in my father's letter, Mr. Brass was the only person still living whom I was able to contact.

2. Harris Peel, *The Trail of 254 thru Blood and Fire* (Gopingen, Germany: J. Kirchner, 1945).

3. James E. Hatcher, *Blood and Fire: With the 63rd Infantry Division in World War II* (n.p.: 63rd Infantry Division Association, 1986).

4. Ibid.

5. Stephen E. Ambrose, *Citizen Soldiers* (New York: Simon & Schuster, 1997); Jeffrey J. Clarke and Robert Ross Smith, *Riviera to the Rhine: European Theatre of Operations* (Honolulu: University Press of the Pacific, 2005). See also Russell Hart and Stephen Hart, *The Second World War (6): Northwest Europe 1944–1945* (Oxford: Osprey, 2002).

6. Carl Brass, telephone interview with author, June 13, 2009.

7. Hatcher, *Blood and Fire,* 5.

8. Peel, *Trail of 254,* 3.

9. Ibid.

10. Hatcher, *Blood and Fire,* 7.

11. Peel, *Trail of 254,* 4.

12. Howard Russell DeMar, "The Sunday Japan Bombed Pearl Harbor," *Blood and Fire* 58, no. 3 (2006): 9.

13. Brass, telephone interview.

14. Peel, *Trail of 254,* 5.

15. Hatcher, *Blood and Fire,* 8.

16. Ibid., 9.

17. Peel, *Trail of 254,* 5.

18. Brass, telephone interview.

19. Peel, *Trail of 254,* 6.

20. Ibid., 7

21. Brass, telephone interview.

22. Hatcher, *Blood and Fire,* 15

23. Hart and Hart, *Second World War,* 7.

24. Clarke and Smith, *Riviera to the Rhine,* 533.

25. Hart and Hart, *Second World War,* 48.

26. Ibid., 51.

27. Ibid.

28. "Visit Alsace," Network Council, accessed July 15, 2009, http://www.visit-alsace.com/where_is_it/index.html.

29. Ambrose, *Citizen Soldiers,* 372.

30. Hatcher, *Blood and Fire,* 20–21.

31. Peel, *Trail of 254,* 12.

32. Ibid.

33. Lyle Atwood, "Sailed Overseas on the SS Saturnia," *Blood and Fire* 60, no. 1 (2008): 33.

34. Peel, *Trail of 254,* 13.

35. Brass, telephone interview.

36. Peel, *Trail of 254,* 14.
37. Peel, *Trail of 254,* 21.
38. Clarke and Smith, *Riviera to the Rhine,* 546.
39. Peel, *Trail of 254,* 27.
40. Hatcher, *Blood and Fire,* 32.
41. Brass, telephone interview.
42. Sixty-third Infantry Division Association (unofficial website), "254th Regimental," accessed February 2, 2012, http://www.63rdinfdiv.com/index1.html.
43. Paul Fussell, *Doing Battle: The Making of a Skeptic* (Boston: Little, Brown, 1996), 160.
44. Peel, *Trail of 254,* 31.
45. Ambrose, *Citizen Soldiers,* 399.
46. Charles D. Rhodes Jr., "Student—Soldier—Survivor," *Blood and Fire* 59, no. 2 (2007): 37.
47. Peel, *Trail of 254,* 35.
48. Ibid.
49. Ibid.
50. Ibid., 36.
51. Hatcher, *Blood and Fire,* 72.
52. Ibid., 73.
53. Hart and Hart, *Second World War,* 55, 58.
54. *Camp Blanding Museum and Memorial Park of the Second World War with Unit Historical Summaries* (Starke, Florida: Florida Army National Guard, 1991), 168–69.
55. Peel, *Trail of 254,* 61.
56. Ibid., 55.
57. Ambrose, *Citizen Soldiers,* 443.
58. Peel, *Trail of 254,* 64.
59. Harry S. Truman, "Message to Congress on Driving for Victory against Japan," 1945. http://www.ibiblio.org/pha/policy/1945/450601a.html.

CHAPTER THREE

1. Portions of this chapter were published previously in Katherine I. Miller, "My Father and His Father: An Analysis of World War II Correspondence," *Journal of Family Communication* 8 (2008), 148–65.
2. Warren Brown, *The Chicago Cubs,* Writing Baseball (Carbondale, Illinois: Southern Illinois University Press, 2001).
3. A telegram reading: "Greetings to the best of fathers. I wish we were together on this special occasion. All my best wishes for a speedy reunion. You are more than ever in my thoughts at this time."
4. See, for example, Walter J. Loesche, Anthony Schork, Margaret S. Terpenning, Yin-Miao Chen, B. Liza Dominguez, and Natalie Grossman, "Assessing the Relation-

ship between Dental Disease and Coronary Heart Disease in Elderly U.S. Veterans," *Journal of the American Dental Association* 129 (1998): 301–311.

5. Judith Parsons, interview with the author, October 26, 2006.

6. Though there had been references to the dental problems, my father clearly thought these were minor issues. Further, actuarial tables indicate that a man of my grandfather's age in 1940 could have expected to live at least twenty more years.

7. See, for example, Michael Scheibach, "Transition to Manhood: Effects of the Great Depression on Male Youth," *Adolescence* 20 (1985): 725–44; Jeffrey Ryan Suzik, "Building Better Men: The CCC Boy and the Changing Social Ideal of Manliness," *Men and Masculinities* 2 (1999): 152–79.

8. Suzik, *Building Better Men,* 168.

9. Steve Meyer, "Rough Manhood: The Aggressive and Confrontational Shop Culture of U.S. Auto Workers during World War II," *Journal of Social History* 36 (2002): 125–47.

10. Christina S. Jarvis, *The Male Body at War: American Masculinity during World War II* (DeKalb, Illinois: Northern Illinois Press, 2004), 8.

11. Susan Faludi, *Stiffed: The Betrayal of the American Man* (New York: HarperCollins, 1999),

12. Margaret Marsh, *Suburban Lives* (New Brunswick, New Jersey: Rutgers University Press, 1990),75.

13. Mark T. Morman and Kory Floyd, "A 'Changing Culture of Fatherhood': Effects on Affectionate Communication, Closeness, and Satisfaction in Men's Relationships with Their Fathers and Their Sons," *Western Journal of Communication* 66 (2002): 396.

14. Dan Kindlon and Michael Thompson, *Raising Cain: Protecting the Emotional Life of Boys* (New York: Random House, 1999).

15. Suni Petersen and Silvia Ecchevaria Rafuls, "Receiving the Scepter: The Generational Transition and Impact of Parent Death on Adults," *Death Studies* 22 (1998): 514.

16. Debra Umberson, *Death of a Parent: Transition into a New Adult Identity* (Cambridge: Cambridge University Press, 2003).

CHAPTER FOUR

1. *The 1943 Rosemary* (Urbana, Illinois: Urbana High School, 1943), 8–9.

2. Caroline is a pseudonym, the only one used in this book. I have used it because Caroline's daughter indicated to me that her mother preferred not to talk about her life and preferred also to remain anonymous. I have respected her wishes.

3. Peter M. Nardi, "'Seamless Souls': An Introduction to Men's Friendships," in *Men's Friendships,* ed. Peter M. Nardi (Newbury Park, California: Sage, 1992), 1–14.

4. Anthony Rotundo, "Romantic Friendships: Male Intimacy and Middle-Class Youth in the Northern United States, 1800–1900," *Journal of Social History* 23 (1989): 1.

5. Victor J. Seidler, "Rejection, Vulnerability, and Friendship," in Nardi, *Men's Friendships,* 15–34.

6. Aristotle, "Rhetoric," in *The Complete Works of Aristotle: The Revised Oxford Translation,* ed. Jonathan Barnes (Princeton: Princeton University Press, 1992), 2:4.

7. Beverly Fehr, *Friendship Processes* (Thousand Oaks, California: Sage, 1996).

8. Scott Feld and William C. Carter, "Foci of Activity as Changing Contexts for Friendship," in *Placing Friendship in Context,* ed. Rebecca G. Adams and Graham Allan (Cambridge: Cambridge University Press, 1998), 136–52.

9. B. Bradford Brown, "A Life-Span Approach to Friendship: Age-Related Dimensions of an Ageless Relationship," in *Research in the Interweave of Social Roles: Friendship,* ed. Helena Z. Lopata and David Maines (Greenwich, Connecticut: JAI Press, 1981), 26.

10. William Broyles Jr., "Why Men Love War," *Esquire,* November 1984. Also available at http://public.wsu.edu/~hughesc/why_men_love_war.htm.

11. Roger Little, "Friendships in the Military Community," in Lopata and Maines, *Research in the Interweave of Social Roles: Friendship,* 230.

12. Claude S. Fischer and Susan L. Phillips, "Who Is Alone? Social Characteristics of People with Small Networks," in *Loneliness: A Sourcebook of Current Theory, Research and Therapy,* ed. Letitia Anne Peplau and Daniel Perlman (New York: Wiley Interscience, 1982), 21–39.

13. Geoffrey L. Greif, *Buddy System* (Oxford: Oxford University Press, 2009).

14. Letty Cottin Pogrebin, *Among Friends: Who We Like, Why We Like Them, and What We Do with Them* (New York: McGraw Hill, 1987), 232.

15. Gary A. Fine, "Friendships in the Workplace," in *Friendship and Social Interaction,* ed. Valerian J. Derlega and Barbara A. Winstead (New York: Springer-Verlag, 1986), 185–206.

16. Fehr, *Friendship Processes,* 47.

17. Lillian B. Rubin, *Just Friends: The Role of Friendship in Our Lives* (New York: Harper & Row, 1985), 61.

18. M. A. Caldwell and Letitia A. Peplau, "Sex Differences in Same-Sex Friendships," *Sex Roles,* 8 (1982): 721–32.

19. Seidler, "Rejection, Vulnerability, and Friendship," 17.

20. Stephen E. Ambrose, *Comrades: Brothers, Fathers, Heroes, Sons, Pals* (Rockland, Massachusetts: Wheeler, 1999), 137–38.

21. Rubin, *Just Friends,* 69.

22. Ibid., 70.

23. J. Glenn Gray, *The Warriors: Reflections on Men in Battle* (Lincoln: University of Nebraska Press,1959), 89–90.

24. See, for example, Theodore F. Cohen, "Men's Families, Men's Friends: A Structural Analysis of Constraints on Men's Social Ties," in Nardi, *Men's Friendships,* 115–31.

25. Barry Wellman, "Men in Networks: Private Communities, Domestic Friendships," in Nardi, *Men's Friendships,* 95.

26. Greif, *Buddy System,* 38.

27. Thomas Childers, *Soldier from the War Returning: The Greatest Generation's Troubled Homecoming from World War II* (Boston: Mariner Books, 2009), 229.

28. Childers, *Soldier from the War,* 258.

CHAPTER FIVE

1. Contemporary scholars have pointed to many of the processes by which children and adolescents can learn about the complexities of working and the workplace. Jennifer Bowes and Jacqueline Goodnow ("Work for Home, School, or Labor Force: The Nature and Sources of Changes in Understanding," *Psychological Bulletin* 119 [1996]: 300–321), point out that one of the most basic of these is by grasping the difference between work and non-work, and that an understanding of the distinction between the two can develop in settings including home, school, and the labor force.

Other scholars discuss the role of part-time employment in organizational socialization and argue that societal changes have made the school system a central location for acquiring occupational knowledge (see Julian Barling, Kimberly-Ann Rogers, and E. Kevin Kelloway, "Some Effects of Teenagers' Part-Time Employment: The Quantity and Quality of Work Make the Difference," *Journal of Organizational Behavior* 16 [1995]: 143–54, and James S. Coleman, "How do the Young Become Adults?," *Review of Educational Research* 42 [1972]: 431–39). For a discussion of the influence of the media on acquisition of workplace skills, see Leah Vande Berg and Nick Trujillo, *Organizational Life on Television* (Norwood, New Jersey: Ablex, 1989).

2. Viktor Gecas, "The Social Psychology of Self-Efficacy," *Annual Review of Sociology* 15 (1989): 291–316.

3. Gretchen M. Spreitzer, "Psychological Empowerment in the Workplace: Dimensions, Measurement, and Validation," *Academy of Management Journal* 38 (1995): 1442–65.

4. Albert Bandura, "Self-Efficacy: Toward a Unifying Theory of Behavioral Change," *Psychological Review* 84 (1977): 191–215.

5. Louis P. Cusella, "Feedback, Motivation, and Performance," in *Handbook of Organizational Communication: An Interdisciplinary Perspective,* ed. Fredrick M. Jablin, Linda L. Putnam, Karlene H. Roberts, and Lyman W. Porter (Newbury Park, California: Sage, 1987), 624–78.

6. Leon Festinger, "A Theory of Social Comparison Processes," *Human Relations* 7 (1954), 117–40.

7. Abraham Maslow, *Motivation and Personality* (New York: Harper & Row, 1954).

8. David D. Franks and Joseph Marolla, "Efficacious Action and Social Approval as Interacting Dimensions of Self-Esteem: A Tentative Formulation through Construct Validation," *Sociometry* 39 (1976): 324–41.

9. Max Weber, *Max Weber: The Theory of Social and Economic Organization,* ed. Talcott Parsons, trans A. M. Henderson (New York: Free Press, 1947).

10. Not surprisingly, my father did not follow through on this threat and accepted

the Bronze Star that was awarded him. It is worth noting, however, that the commendation states that the award was given because of his diligent and dangerous work in supporting the efforts of a superior officer.

11. Peter S. Kindsvatter, *American Soldiers: Ground Combat in the World Wars, Korea, and Vietnam* (Lawrence: University of Kansas Press, 2003), 248.

12. James W. Dean Jr., Pamela Brandes, and Ravi Dharwadkar, "Organizational Cynicism," *Academy of Management Review* 23 (1998): 345.

13. Rebecca Abraham, "Organizational Cynicism: Bases and Consequences," *Genetic, Social, and General Psychology Monographs* 126, no. 3 (2000): 270.

14. Walter D. Davis and William L. Gardner, "Perceptions of Politics and Organizational Cynicism: An Attributional and Leader-Member Exchange Perspective,"*Leadership Quarterly* 15 (2004): 439–65.

15. See, for example, Jeanne M. McGee and Jean Stockard, "From a Child's View: Children's Occupational Knowledge and Perceptions of Occupational Characteristics," in *Sociological Studies of Child Development,* ed. Nancy Mandell (Greenwich, Connecticut: JAI Press, 1991), 113–36.

16. Kenneth J. Levine and Cynthia A. Hoffner, "Adolescents' Conceptions of Work: What Is Learned from Different Sources during Anticipatory Socialization?," *Journal of Adolescent Research* 21 (2006): 647–69.

17. George H. Douglas, *The Golden Age of the Newspaper* (Westport, Connecticut: Greenwood Press, 1999), ix.

18. Fred Fedler, *Lessons from the Past: Journalists' Lives and Work, 1850—1950* (Prospect Heights, Illinois: Waveland Press, 2000), 12.

19. Russell Baker, *The Good Times* (New York: William Morrow, 1989), 51.

20. My father strongly believed later in his life in the importance of journalism in enhancing community and democracy. In a 1978 letter to my sister Mary, he extolled the virtues of "The Press" as a "helping field." He told her: "It is my belief that the press has done more for this country than any other institution. From Tom Paine to Woodstein, it has made this country possible."

21. Roger Little, "Friendships in the Military Community," in *Research in the Interweave of Social Roles: Friendship,* ed. Helena Z. Lopata and David Maines (Greenwich, Connecticut: JAI Press, 1981), 231.

22. Kindsvatter, *American Soldiers,* 101.

23. Ibid., 102.

24. Willard Walter Waller, *The Veteran Comes Back* (New York: Dryden Press, 1944).

25. Michael D. Gambone, *The Greatest Generation Comes Home: The Veteran in American Society* (College Station: Texas A&M University Press, 2005), 30.

26. Ibid., 64.

27. Ibid., 68.

28. Ibid., 72.

29. For a description of typical tasks of newspaper copy editors, see Bill Walsh,

"The Lot of Journalism's Noble Misfits," accessed November 19, 2009, http://www.theslot.com/copyeditors.html.

30. See, for example, Charles W. Madigan, *-30-: The Collapse of the Great American Newspaper* (Chicago: Ivan R. Dee, 2007).

CHAPTER SIX

1. See Bernard Gert, "The Definition of Morality," *Stanford Encyclopedia of Philosophy,* ed. Edward N. Zalta, Fall 2008 ed., accessed December 1, 2009, http://plato.stanford.edu/.

2. Elliot Turiel, "Thought, Emotions, and Social Interactional Processes in Moral Development," in *Handbook of Moral Development,* ed. Melanie Killen and Judith Smetana (Mahwah, New Jersey: Lawrence Erlbaum, 2006), 13.

3. Lawrence Kohlberg, *Essays on Moral Development,* vol. 1 of *The Philosophy of Moral Development* (San Francisco: Harper & Row, 1981).

4. Paul Fussell, *Wartime: Understanding and Behavior in the Second World War* (Oxford: Oxford University Press, 1989), 96.

5. Bill Mauldin, *Up Front* (New York: Award Books, 1976), 89–90.

6. Charles Stangor and Mark Schaller, "Stereotypes as Individual and Collective Representations," in *Foundations of Stereotypes and Stereotyping,* ed. C. Neil Macrae, Miles Hewstone, and Charles Stangor (New York: Guilford, 1996), 3–37.

7. Stephen E. Ambrose, *Citizen Soldiers* (New York: Simon & Schuster, 1997), 443.

8. In 1932, college students in one sample were most likely to describe "Jews" as shrewd (79%), mercenary (49%), industrious (48%), grasping (34%), and intelligent (29%). In 1950, these response percentages had shifted substantially (shrewd—47%, mercenary—28%, industrious—29%, intelligent—37%) (G. M. Gilbert, "Stereotype Persistence and Change among College Students," *Journal of Abnormal and Social Psychology* 46 [1951]: 245–54).

9. Fussell, *Wartime,* 115.

10. Ibid., 70.

11. See Bruce Bower, "Fighting Stereotype Stigma: Studies Chart Accuracy, Usefulness of Inferences about Social Groups," *Science News,* June 29, 1996, 408.

12. Ibid. See also Yueh-Ting Lee, Lee J. Jussim, and Clark McCauley, eds., *Stereotype Accuracy: Toward Appreciating Group Differences* (Washington, DC: American Psychological Association, 1995).

13. Fussell, *Wartime,* 67.

14. Peter S. Kindsvatter, *American Soldiers: Ground Combat in the World Wars, Korea, & Vietnam* (Lawrence: University of Kansas Press, 2003), 136–37.

15. Fussell, *Wartime,* 279.

16. Ibid., 145.

17. Weeks later, on January 29, 1945, *Stars and Stripes* reported under the headline "Says He Said GIs DO Want to Go Home" that Representative John E. Sheridan

(D-Pennsylvania) was misquoted. "His correct comment, he asserted, was that of about 1,500,000 Americans fighting Germany, 'I didn't find 100 who wouldn't give up their rotation or furlough home if they felt it would end the war one day sooner."

18. Eric J. Leed, *No Man's Land: Combat and Identity in World War I* (Cambridge: Cambridge University Press, 1979).

19. James Bradley, *Flags of Our Fathers: Heroes of Iwo Jima* (New York: Delacourt, 2001), 10.

20. J. Glenn Gray, *The Warriors: Reflections on Men in Battle* (Lincoln: University of Nebraska Press, 1959).

21. Ibid., 119. See also Peter S. Kindsvatter, *American Soldiers: Ground Combat in the World Wars, Korea, & Vietnam* (Lawrence: University of Kansas Press, 2003), who argues that "soldiers who arrived on the battlefield with 'this-world' faith . . . went through a painful process of questioning, and sometimes rejecting, their belief" (116).

22. Carol Gilligan, *In a Different Voice: Psychological Theory and Women's Development* (Cambridge: Harvard University Press, 1982).

EPILOGUE

1. "Bestselling Books of the Year, 1996–2007," March 24, 2008, accessed January 14, 2010, http://www.publishersweekly.com.

2. Kenneth D. Rose, *Myth and the Greatest Generation: A Social History of Americans in World War II* (New York: Routledge, 2008), 2.

3. Tom Brokaw, *The Greatest Generation* (New York: Random House, 1998); Tom Brokaw, *The Greatest Generation Speaks: Letters and Reflections* (New York: Random House, 1999); Tom Brokaw, *An Album of Memories: Personal Histories from the Greatest Generation* (New York: Random House, 2001).

4. Brokaw, *Greatest Generation,* xix–xx.

5. Rod Gragg, *From Foxholes and Flight Decks: Letters Home from World War II* (New York: St. Martin's, 2002), 13.

6. Tom Mathews, *Our Fathers' War: Growing Up in the Shadow of the Greatest Generation* (New York: Broadway Books, 2005).

7. Denise M. Bostdorff, "George W. Bush's Post-September 11 Rhetoric of Covenant Renewal: Upholding the Faith of the Greatest Generation," *Quarterly Journal of Speech* 89 (2003): 299.

8. George W. Bush, "Remarks at the United Nations General Assembly in New York City" (New York, November 10, 2001), http://www.september11news.com/PresidentBushUN.htm.

9. Brokaw, *Greatest Generation,* 293.

10. Rose, *Myth and the Greatest Generation,* 3.

11. Thomas Childers, *Soldier from the War Returning: The Greatest Generation's Troubled Homecoming from World War II* (Boston: Mariner Books, 2009), 4.

12. Michael C. C. Adams, *The Best War Ever* (Baltimore: Johns Hopkins University Press, 1994), 9.

13. Ibid., 11.

14. Ibid., 15.

15. Ibid., 2.

16. James Jones, *The Thin Red Line* (New York: Delta, 1998); Norman Mailer, *The Naked and the Dead* (New York: Rinehart, 1948).

17. Rose, *Myth and the Greatest Generation;* Adams, *Best War Ever;* Childers, *Soldier from the War Returning;* Gerald F. Linderman, *The World within War: America's Combat Experiences in World War II* (New York: Free Press, 1997).

18. John Whiteclay Chambers, "Book Review of Kenneth D. Rose's *Myth and the Greatest Generation,*" *American Historical Review* 113, no. 3 (June 2009), 786.

19. Studs Terkel, *"The Good War": An Oral History of World War II* (New York: New Press, 1984).

20. See, for example, Edward T. Richardson, Jr., *Blood and Candles: The Story of a World War II Infantryman* (Victoria, British Columbia: Trafford Press, 2002) and Julia Collins, *My Father's War* (New York: Four Walls Eight Windows, 2002).

21. Paul Fussell, *The Boys' Crusade: The American Infantry in Northwestern Europe, 1944–1945* (New York: Random House, 2003); Paul Fussell, *Wartime: Understanding and Behavior in the Second World War* (Oxford: Oxford University Press, 1989); Paul Fussell, *Doing Battle: The Making of a Skeptic* (Boston: Little, Brown, 1996).

22. Fussell, *Doing Battle,* 9.

23. Ibid., 169.

24. Ibid., 296.

BIBLIOGRAPHY

Abraham, Rebecca. "Organizational Cynicism: Bases and Consequences." *Genetic, Social, and General Psychology Monographs* 126, no. 3 (2000): 269–92.

Adams, Michael C. C. *The Best War Ever.* Baltimore: Johns Hopkins University Press, 1994.

Adler, Bill, with Tracy Quinn McLennan, eds. *World War II Letters.* New York: St Martin's, 2002.

Ambrose, Stephen E. *Citizen Soldiers.* New York: Simon & Schuster, 1997.

———. *Comrades: Brothers, Fathers, Heroes, Sons, Pals.* Rockland, Massachusetts: Wheeler, 1999.

Aristotle. "Rhetoric." In *The Complete Works of Aristotle: The Revised Oxford Translation,* edited by Jonathan Barnes, 2:2159–2269. Princeton: Princeton University Press, 1992.

Atwood, Lyle. "Sailed Overseas on the SS Saturnia." *Blood and Fire* 60, no. 1 (2008): 32–33.

Baker, Russell. *The Good Times.* New York: William Morrow, 1989.

Bandura, Albert. "Self-Efficacy: Toward a Unifying Theory of Behavioral Change." *Psychological Review* 84 (1977): 191–215.

Barling, Julian, Kimberly-Ann Rogers, and E. Kevin Kelloway. "Some Effects of Teenagers' Part-Time Employment: The Quantity and Quality of Work Make the Difference." *Journal of Organizational Behavior* 16 (1995): 143–54.

Bostdorff, Denise M. "George W. Bush's Post-September 11 Rhetoric of Covenant Renewal: Upholding the Faith of the Greatest Generation." *Quarterly Journal of Speech* 89 (2003): 293–319.

Bower, Bruce. "Fighting Stereotype Stigma: Studies Chart Accuracy, Usefulness of Inferences about Social Groups." *Science News,* June 29, 1996, 408.

Bowes, Jennifer M., and Jacqueline J. Goodnow. "Work for Home, School, or Labor Force: The Nature and Sources of Changes in Understanding." *Psychological Bulletin* 119 (1996): 300–321.

Bradley, James. *Flags of Our Fathers: Heroes of Iwo Jima.* New York: Delacourt, 2001.

Brokaw, Tom. *An Album of Memories: Personal Histories from the Greatest Generation.* New York: Random House, 2001.

———. *The Greatest Generation.* New York: Random House, 1998.

———. *The Greatest Generation Speaks: Letters and Reflections.* New York: Random House, 1999.

Brown, B. Bradford. "A Life-Span Approach to Friendship: Age-Related Dimensions of an Ageless Relationship." In *Research in the Interweave of Social Roles: Friendship,* edited by Helena Z. Lopata and David Maines, 23–50. Greenwich, Connecticut: JAI Press, 1981.

Brown, Warren. *The Chicago Cubs.* Writing Baseball. Carbondale, Illinois: Southern Illinois University Press, 2001.

Broyles, William, Jr. "Why Men Love War." *Esquire,* November 1984.

Caldwell, M. A., and Letitia Anne Peplau. "Sex Differences in Same-Sex Friendships." *Sex Roles* 8 (1982): 721–32.

Camp Blanding Museum and Memorial Park of the Second World War with Unit Historical Summaries. Starke, Florida: Florida Army National Guard, 1991.

Carroll, Andrew, ed. *War Letters: Extraordinary Correspondence from American Wars.* New York: Washington Square, 2001.

Caulfield, L. M. "Birth and Death of a World War II Army Camp—Camp Van Dorn, Mississippi." 63rd Infantry Division (unofficial site). Accessed November 18, 2009. http://www.63rdinfdiv.com/historyvandornpage1.html.

Chambers, John Whiteclay, II. Review of *Myth and the Greatest Generation,"* by Kenneth D. Rose. *American Historical Review* 113, no. 3 (June 2009): 786–87.

———, ed. *The Oxford Companion to American Military History* (Oxford: Oxford University Press, 1999).

Childers, Thomas. *Soldier from the War Returning: The Greatest Generation's Troubled Homecoming from World War II.* Boston: Mariner Books, 2009.

Clarke, Jeffrey J., and Robert Ross Smith. *Riviera to the Rhine: European Theatre of Operations.* Honolulu: University Press of the Pacific, 2005.

Cohen, Theodore F. "Men's Families, Men's Friends: A Structural Analysis of Constraints on Men's Social Ties." In *Men's Friendships,* edited by Peter M. Nardi, 115–31. Newbury Park, California: Sage, 1992.

Coleman, James S. "How Do the Young Become Adults?" *Review of Educational Research* 42 (1972): 431–39.

Collins, Julia. *My Father's War.* New York: Four Walls Eight Windows, 2002.

Cussella, Louis P. "Feedback, Motivation, and Performance." In *Handbook of Organizational Communication: An Interdisciplinary Perspective,* edited by Fredrick M. Jablin, Linda L. Putnam, Karlene H. Roberts, and Lyman W. Porter, 624–78. Newbury Park, California: Sage, 1987.

Davis, Walter D., and William L. Gardner. "Perceptions of Politics and Organizational Cynicism: An Attributional and Leader-Member Exchange Perspective." *Leadership Quarterly* 15 (2004): 439–65.

Dean, James W., Jr., Pamela Brandes, and Ravi Dharwadkar. "Organizational Cynicism." *Academy of Management Review* 23 (1998): 341–52.

DeMar, Howard Russell. "The Sunday Japan Bombed Pearl Harbor." *Blood and Fire* 58, no. 3 (2006).

Denzin, Norman K. *Interpretive Biography.* Newbury Park, California: Sage, 1989.

Douglas, George H. *The Golden Age of the Newspaper.* Westport, Connecticut: Greenwood Press, 1999.

Elder, Glen H., Jr. "War Mobilization and the Life Course: A Cohort of World War II Veterans." *Sociological Forum* 2 (1987): 449–72.

Faludi, Susan. *Stiffed: The Betrayal of the American Man.* New York: HarperCollins, 1999.

Fedler, Fred. *Lessons from the Past: Journalists' Lives and Work, 1850–1950.* Prospect Heights, Illinois: Waveland, 2000.

Fehr, Beverly. *Friendship Processes.* Thousand Oaks, California: Sage, 1996.

Feld, Scott, and William C. Carter. "Foci of Activity as Changing Contexts for Friendship." In *Placing Friendship in Context,* edited by Rebecca G. Adams and Graham Allan, 136–52. Cambridge: Cambridge University Press, 1998.

Festinger, Leon. "A Theory of Social Comparison Processes." *Human Relations* 7 (1954): 117–40.

Fine, Gary A. "Friendships in the Workplace." In *Friendship and Social Interaction,* edited by Valerian J. Derlega and Barbara A. Winstead, 185–206. New York: Springer-Verlag, 1986.

Fischer, Claude S., and Susan L. Phillips. "Who Is Alone? Social Characteristics of People with Small Networks." In *Loneliness: A Sourcebook of Current Theory, Research, and Therapy,* edited by Letitia Anne Peplau and Daniel Perlman, 21–39. New York: Wiley Interscience, 1982.

Franks, David D., and Joseph Marolla. "Efficacious Action and Social Approval as Interacting Dimensions of Self-Esteem: A Tentative Formulation through Construct Validation." *Sociometry* 39 (1976): 324–41.

Freedman, Russell. *Children of the Great Depression.* New York: Clarion Books, 2005.

Fussell, Paul. *The Boys' Crusade: The American Infantry in Northwestern Europe, 1944—1945.* New York: Random House, 2003.

———. *Doing Battle: The Making of a Skeptic.* Boston: Little, Brown, 1996.

———. *Wartime: Understanding and Behavior in the Second World War.* Oxford: Oxford University Press, 1989.

Gambone, Michael D. *The Greatest Generation Comes Home: The Veteran in American Society.* College Station: Texas A&M University Press, 2005.

Gecas, Viktor. "The Social Psychology of Self-Efficacy." *Annual Review of Sociology* 15 (1989): 291–316.

Gert, Bernard. "The Definition of Morality." In *The Stanford Encyclopedia of Philosophy,* edited by Edward N. Zalta. 2008 ed. http://plato.stanford.edu/archives/fall2008/entries/morality-definition/.

Gilbert, G. M. "Stereotype Persistence and Change among College Students." *Journal of Abnormal and Social Psychology* 46 (1951): 245–54.

Gilligan, Carol. *In a Different Voice: Psychological Theory and Women's Development.* Cambridge, Massachusetts: Harvard University Press, 1982.

Goodall, H. Lloyd. *A Need to Know: A Clandestine History of a CIA Family.* Walnut Creek, California: Left Coast, 2006.

Gragg, Rod. *From Foxholes and Flight Decks: Letters Home from World War II.* New York: St. Martin's, 2002.

Gray, J. Glenn. *The Warriors: Reflections on Men in Battle.* Lincoln: University of Nebraska Press, 1959.

Greif, Geoffrey L. *Buddy System.* Oxford: Oxford University Press, 2009.

Hart, Russell, and Stephen Hart. *The Second World War (6): Northwest Europe 1944–1945.* Oxford: Osprey, 2002.

Hatcher, James E. *Blood and Fire: With the 63rd Infantry Division in World War II.* N.p.: 63rd Infantry Division Association, 1986.

Havighurst, Robert, G., John W. Baughman, Ernest W. Burgess, and Walter H. Eaton. *The American Veteran Back Home: A Study of Veteran Readjustment.* New York: Longsman, Green, 1951.

Jarvis, Christina S. *The Male Body at War: American Masculinity during World War II.* DeKalb, Illinois: Northern Illinois University Press, 2004.

Jones, James. *The Thin Red Line.* New York: Delta, 1998.

Kindlon, Dan, and Michael Thompson. *Raising Cain: Protecting the Emotional Life of Boys.* New York: Random House, 1999.

Kindsvatter, Peter S. *American Soldiers: Ground Combat in the World Wars, Korea, and Vietnam.* Lawrence, Kansas: University of Kansas Press, 2003.

Kohlberg, Lawrence. *The Philosophy of Moral Development.* Vol. 1 of *Essays on Moral Development.* San Francisco: Harper & Row, 1981.

Kotlowitz, Robert. *Before Their Time.* New York: Anchor Books, 1997.

Lee, Yueh-Ting, Lee J. Jussim, and Clark McCauley, eds. *Stereotype Accuracy: Toward Appreciating Group Differences.* Washington, DC: American Psychological Association, 1995.

Leed, Eric J. *No Man's Land: Combat and Identity in World War I.* Cambridge: Cambridge University Press, 1979.

Levine, Kenneth J., and Cynthia A. Hoffner. "Adolescents' Conceptions of Work: What Is Learned from Different Sources during Anticipatory Socialization?" *Journal of Adolescent Research* 21 (2006): 647–69.

Linderman, Gerald F. *The World within War: America's Combat Experiences in World War II.* New York: Free Press, 1997.

Little, Roger. "Friendships in the Military Community." In *Research in the Interweave of Social Roles: Friendship,* edited by Helena Z. Lopata and David Maines, 221–35. Greenwich, Connecticut: JAI Press, 1981.

Loesche, Walter J., Anthony Schork, Margaret S. Terpenning, Yin-Miao Chen, B. Liza Dominguez, and Natalie Grossman. "Assessing the Relationship between Dental Disease and Coronary Heart Disease in Elderly U.S. Veterans." *Journal of the American Dental Association* 129 (1998): 301–311.

Madigan, Charles W. *-30-: The Collapse of the Great American Newspaper.* Chicago: Ivan R. Dee, 2007.

Mailer, Norman. *The Naked and the Dead.* New York: Rinehart, 1948.

Marsh, Margaret. *Suburban Lives.* New Brunswick, New Jersey: Rutgers University Press, 1990.

Maslow, Abraham. *Motivation and Personality.* New York: Harper & Row, 1954.

Mathews, Tom. *Our Fathers' War: Growing Up in the Shadow of the Greatest Generation.* New York: Broadway Books, 2005.

Mauldin, Bill. *Up Front.* New York: Award, 1976.

McGee, Jeanne M. and Jean Stockard. "From a Child's View: Children's Occupational Knowledge and Perceptions of Occupational Characteristics." In *Sociological Studies of Child Development,* edited by Nancy Mandell, 113–36. Greenwich, Connecticut: JAI Press, 1991.

Meyer, Steve. "Rough Manhood: The Aggressive and Confrontational Shop Culture of U.S. Auto Workers during World War II." *Journal of Social History* 36 (2002): 125–47.

Miller, Katherine I. "My Father and His Father: An Analysis of World War II Correspondence." *Journal of Family Communication* 8 (2008), 148–65.

Morman, Mark T., and Kory Floyd. "A 'Changing Culture of Fatherhood': Effects on Affectionate Communication, Closeness, and Satisfaction in Men's Relationships with Their Fathers and Their Sons." *Western Journal of Communication* 66 (2002): 395–411.

Nardi, Peter M. "'Seamless Souls': An Introduction to Men's Friendships." In *Men's Friendships,* edited by Peter M. Nardi, 1–14. Newbury Park, California: Sage, 1992.

O'Brien, Tim. *The Things They Carried.* New York: Penguin, 1990.

Obermayer, Herbert J. *Soldiering for Freedom.* College Station: Texas A&M University Press, 2005.

Peel, Harris. *The Trail of 254 thru Blood and Fire.* Gopingen, Germany: J. Kirchner, 1945.

Petersen, Suni, and Silvia Ecchevaria Rafuls. "Receiving the Scepter: The Generational Transition and Impact of Parent Death on Adults." *Death Studies* 22 (1998): 493–524.

Pfeiffer, Don. *IRTC Handbook: Camp Blanding, Florida.* Camp Blanding, Florida: Special Service IRTC, n.d.

Pogrebin, Letty Cottin. *Among Friends: Who We Like, Why We Like Them, and What We Do with Them.* New York: McGraw Hill, 1987.

Pyle, Ernie. "The God-Damned Infantry." *Reporting America at War.* PBS. Accessed November 18, 2009. www.pbs.org/weta/reportingamericaatwar/reporters/infantry.html.

Rhodes, Charles D., Jr. "Student—Soldier—Survivor." *Blood and Fire* 59, no. 2 (2007): 33–46.

Richardson, Edward T., Jr. *Blood and Candles: The Story of a World War II Infantryman.* Victoria, British Columbia: Trafford Press, 2002.

Rose, Kenneth D. *Myth and the Greatest Generation: A Social History of Americans in World War II.* New York: Routledge, 2008.

Rotundo, Anthony. "Romantic Friendships: Male Intimacy and Middle-Class Youth in the Northern United States, 1800–1900." *Journal of Social History* 23 (1989): 1–25.

Rubin, Lillian B. *Just Friends: The Role of Friendship in Our Lives.* New York: Harper & Row, 1985.

Rush, Robert S. *The US Infantryman in World War II.* Oxford: Osprey, 2003.

Scheibach, Michael. "Transition to Manhood: Effects of the Great Depression on Male Youth." *Adolescence* 20 (1985): 725–44.

Seidler, Victor J., "Rejection, Vulnerability, and Friendship." In *Men's Friendships,* edited by Peter M. Nardi, 15–34. Newbury Park, California: Sage, 1992.

Spreitzer, Gretchen M. "Psychological Empowerment in the Workplace: Dimensions, Measurement, and Validation." *Academy of Management Journal* 38 (1995): 1442–65.

Stangor, Charles, and Mark Schaller. "Stereotypes as Individual and Collective Representations." In *Foundations of Stereotypes and Stereotyping,* edited by C. Neil Macrae, Miles Hewstone, and Charles Stangor, 3–37. New York: Guilford, 1996.

Suzik, Jeffrey Ryan. "Building Better Men: The CCC Boy and the Changing Social Ideal of Manliness." *Men and Masculinities* 2 (1999): 152–72.

Terkel, Studs. *"The Good War": An Oral History of World War II.* New York: New Press, 1984.

Trujillo, Nick. *In Search of Naunny's Grave: Age, Class, Gender, and Ethnicity in an American Family.* Walnut Creek, California: AltaMira, 2004.

Truman, Harry S. "Message to Congress on Driving for Victory against Japan." June 1, 1945. http://www.ibiblio.org/pha/policy/1945/450601a.html.

Turiel, Ellio. "Thought, Emotions, and Social Interaction in Moral Development." In *Handbook of Moral Development,* edited by Melanie Killen and Judith Smetana, 7–35. Mahwah, New Jersey: Lawrence Erlbaum, 2006.

Umberson, Debra. *Death of a Parent: Transition into a New Adult Identity.* Cambridge: Cambridge University Press, 2003.

Vande Berg, Leah, and Nick Trujillo. *Organizational Life on Television.* Norwood, New Jersey: Ablex, 1989.

Van Dorn Army Museum. *History.* Accessed November 18, 2009. http://www.vandornmuseum.org.

Waller, Willard Walter. *The Veteran Comes Back.* New York: Dryden Press, 1944.

Walsh, Bill. "The Lot of Journalism's Noble Misfits." Accessed November 19, 2009. http://www.theslot.com/copyeditors.html.

Weber, Max. *Max Weber: The Theory of Social and Economic Organization.* Edited by Talcott Parsons. Translated by A. M. Henderson. New York: Free Press, 1947.

Wellman, Barry. "Men in Networks: Private Communities, Domestic Friendships." In *Men's Friendships,* edited by Peter M. Nardi, 74–114. Newbury Park, California: Sage, 1992.

INDEX